DIFFICULT
FUNERAL SERVICES

BY James L. Christensen

Funeral Services
The Minister's Service Handbook
The Minister's Marriage Handbook
The Complete Funeral Manual
Funeral Services for Today
The Minister's Church, Home, and
  Community Services Handbook
Before Saying "I Do"
Difficult Funeral Services

DIFFICULT FUNERAL SERVICES

James L. Christensen

Fleming H. Revell Company
Old Tappan, New Jersey

Library of Congress Cataloging in Publication Data

Christensen, James L.
  Difficult funeral services.

  Bibliography: p.
  1. Funeral service.   2. Funeral sermons.   I. Title.
BV199.F8C49   1985   265'.85   84-15072
ISBN 0-8007-1218-8

Contents

69760

6   *Contents*

DIFFICULT FUNERAL SERVICES

FOR A STRANGER

Prelude

"When All My Labors and Trials Are O'er"
"Face to Face With Christ, My Savior"

Opening Sentences

"Oh, it's only Joe!"
   They said.
Only?
   Can anyone be only?[1]

Invocation

O God our Father, who created us human beings in Your likeness, male and female You created us, to have dominion over all creatures of earth; You looked at all you created and said, "Behold, it is very good"; You sacrificed Your own Son for our welfare; we rejoice and are gladdened that no one is a nobody to You, no one is a stranger to You, and no one is ever beyond Your love. Lift up our hearts. Yea, we lift them up, O Lord.

Hymn (optional)

"What a Friend We Have in Jesus"

Old Testament Scripture Readings

General Selections:
Psalm 23
Genesis 1:1–5, 24–28, 31

Specifically Relevant Selection:

> O Lord our Lord, how excellent is thy name in all
> the earth! . . . When I consider thy heavens, the work
> of thy fingers, the moon and the stars, which thou
> hast ordained; What is man, that thou art mindful of
> him? and the son of man, that thou visitest him? . . .
> O Lord our Lord, how excellent is thy name in all the
> earth!
>
> Psalms 8:1, 3, 4, 9

New Testament Scripture Readings

General Selection:
Philippians 4:8, 9

Specifically Relevant Selection:

> Now therefore ye are no more strangers and
> foreigners, but fellowcitizens with the saints, and of
> the household of God; And are built upon the foun-
> dation of the apostles and prophets, Jesus Christ
> himself being the chief corner stone; In whom all the
> building fitly framed together groweth unto an holy
> temple in the Lord: In whom ye also are builded to-
> gether for an habitation of God through the Spirit.
>
> Ephesians 2:19–22

Pastoral Prayer

Lord, God, we are comforted by the Holy Scripture readings, which speak Your thoughts to our minds and Your love
to our hearts.

To these dear people who feel the pangs of separation, Lord,
grant resources of spirit to assimilate this loss—gratitude for
the life that has been lived among them, forgiveness to assuage
the feelings of guilt and remorse, faith in the invisible realities,
peace in the distribution of estate and renewed commitment to
Your will in life.

What honor is due this loved one. May there surface in the

minds of these mourning his death, that which was good and honorable. May the shortcomings and failures kindly melt from their memories, to be reckoned from Your perspective and wisdom.

Let us so live that when our summons calls, we may be prepared to meet our Maker, through Jesus Christ, our Anchor of Hope. Amen.

Hymn (optional)

"Spirit of God, Descend Upon My Heart"

Meditation

REMEMBERING THE GOOD

The prophet Nehemiah concludes the writing that bears his name with a beautiful prayer—one of the most beautiful in all Scripture—one that all of us should pray. Here it is: ". . . Remember me, O my God, for good" (Nehemiah 13:31).

This was Nehemiah's earnest plea and desire above all others—that when his life was finished he would be remembered "for good."

We do remember different people for different things. Mention Moses, and you think of his delivering the children of Israel from Egyptian slavery. Mention David, and you remember his slaying a giant with a slingshot.

Memory is the stretch of the mind reaching across the years. One of the unique capacities of the human being is the ability to remember. It derives from God, who remembers.

We are here in memory of _____. How will he be remembered by his family? By his neighbors? By his working associates? By his community? Above all, how will God, His Creator, remember him? That is the crucial question.

All of you have known him better than have I. The details of his life and relationships I do not know. This I do know—in every man and woman there is some good—it may not always predominate; it may be vague; but in every person—even those who seem scoundrels, there is good.

I bid you today to seek out the good in this person's character and life. Be gentle and forgiving of the weaknesses and failures; let them slip into the forgotten; then paint firmly on the canvas of your mind that which you loved, that which was well intentioned, and the deeds of unselfishness.

Jesus, who revealed God's attitudes, always saw deeply into people's lives to see the good there. He did not condemn Peter for his weakness; He appealed to his strength and developed his character. Peter became a good man of good works. Nathaniel was a prejudiced, hot-blooded bigot who said, "Nothing good can come out of Nazareth." He did not love Jesus, but Jesus loved him. Jesus saw his good, and Nathaniel became transformed. He did not condemn Mary Magdalene, the woman of the streets; He forgave her and believed in her potential when no one else looked quite far enough to see it.

How unlike Jesus we are. We look for the bad; we dwell on the weaknesses; we lose sight of the good and the struggle and the valiant effort.

We come here today to focus on the good in the character, works, and life of _____, remembering the admonition of the Apostle Paul,

> ... Whatever is true,
> Whatever is honorable,
> Whatever is just,
> Whatever is pure,
> Whatever is lovely,
> Whatever is gracious,
> if there is any excellence, if there is anything worthy
> of praise, *think* about these things.
>
> Philippians 4:8 RSV, *italics mine*

To his friend Philemon, the Apostle wrote, "I thank my God always when I remember you . . ." (Philemon 4). Just so, we lift to God our gratitude for the good we remember in our departed.

May we so live that the prayer can be answered affirmatively, "Remember me, O my God, for good!"

Benediction

Now may the peace of God which passes all understanding abide in your hearts to give you comfort and keep you in union with Jesus Christ, now and forever. Amen.

Postlude

"Guide Me, O Thou Great Jehovah"

2

FOR A TEENAGE DRUG ADDICT

Prelude

"They That Wait Upon the Lord"
"When All My Labors and Trials Are O'er"

Opening Sentences

This I Know

Only for a little space
Songs of joy are still—
Only through a midnight's watch
Shall our tears be spilled.

Only for a little while
Cloud-banks will be dark,
Then will fingers, quite unseen,
Paint the rainbow's arc.

This I know, though gleaming threads
Of our lives be crossed,
Yet a space and we shall find
Songs we thought were lost.[1]

Invocation

O God of light eternal, beyond the clouds and darkness of this day, we look to Thee for Thy never-failing light. Thou art our Father, our Helper, our Hope. Give us the assurance that what has brought us bereavement has meant release and peace to our loved one, through Jesus Christ, our Lord. Amen.

Hymn (optional)

"The Lord's Prayer"
"The Lord Is My Shepherd"

Old Testament Scripture Readings

General Selections:
   Psalms 39:5–8, 12
   Psalms 46:5
   Psalms 51:1–3, 7–12
   Psalms 139:3, 17, 18

New Testament Scripture Readings

General Selections:
   1 John 4:7–13
   1 John 4:16–21

Specifically Relevant Selections:

> If I speak in the tongues of men and of angels, but have not love, I am a noisy gong or a clanging cymbal. And if I have prophetic powers, and understand all mysteries and all knowledge, and if I have all faith, so as to remove mountains, but have not love, I am nothing. If I give away all I have, and if I deliver my body to be burned, but have not love, I gain nothing.
>
> Love is patient and kind; love is not jealous or boastful; it is not arrogant or rude. Love does not in-

sist on its own way; it is not irritable or resentful; it does not rejoice at wrong, but rejoices in the right. Love bears all things, believes all things, hopes all things, endures all things.

Love never ends; as for prophecies, they will pass away; as for tongues, they will cease; as for knowledge, it will pass away. For our knowledge is imperfect and our prophecy is imperfect; but when the perfect comes, the imperfect will pass away. When I was a child, I spoke like a child, I thought like a child, I reasoned like a child; when I became a man, I gave up childish ways. For now we see in a mirror dimly, but then face to face. Now I know in part; then I shall understand fully, even as I have been fully understood. So faith, hope, love abide, these three; but the greatest of these is love.

1 Corinthians 13 RSV

If we say that we have no sin, we deceive ourselves, and the truth is not in us. If we confess our sins, he is faithful and just to forgive us our sins, and to cleanse us from all unrighteousness. If we say that we have not sinned, we make him a liar, and his word is not in us.

1 John 1:8–10

Pastoral Prayer

Speak to us Thy forgiving love, O God. As we bring ourselves into Your presence, have mercy upon us, gracious Father, and upon _____, as we commend him to your care.

Dear God, tenderly comfort these bereaved friends. May they find in You their solace and strength. Deliver them from bitterness and despair.

Remembering the words of Jesus, "Whoever comes to me, I will not cast out," we plead Your forgiveness. Too much we have ignored our neighbor's needs, lived as if there were no God, and have not heeded the call of the deep echoing in the canyons of time. Have mercy, O Lord.

Now that our hearts are opened and our spirits quickened, speak to us of eternal matters, strengthen our wills in Yours, challenge us in ways to make our youth safe, fill our minds with peace so that we may resolutely live for Him who died for us. Thanks be unto You, O God.

Hymn (optional)

"God So Loved the World"
"Beautiful Saviour"
"Fairest Lord Jesus"

Meditation

NOW IS THE TIME FOR LOVE

Love
Love is glad when you are glad
Is sad when you are sad
Is hurt when you are.
Love is never so wrapped in self,
That it can't listen to you,
And hear you. . . .
Love knows no time
And is always available.
Love . . . looks with you
For the right path for you.
Love makes no judgments
And has a deep respect for you;
Love grows by sharing . . .
Love drives out fear;
Love is eternal and never dies,
Love cares.[2]

"God is love." That is the best definition of God we know. "For God so loved the world that he gave his only Son, that whoever believes in him should not perish but have eternal life" (John 3:16 RSV). "We love, because he first loved us" (1 John 4:19 RSV).

The Bible in many ways assures us of God's love: by a shepherd who hunted all over a mountain range to find one lost sheep; by a father who received back a rebellious son who violated his trust, squandered a fortune, and broke his parent's heart; by one named Jesus, who laid down His life upon the cross to reclaim willful, misguided people.

At the heart of existence is love. God has made no one in vain and no one whom He does not love. He loves us. No one is ever beyond His love. How comforting is that assurance!

"We love, because he first loved us." "By this all men will know that you are my disciples, if you have love for one another," said Jesus (John 13:35 RSV).

So we have come here in love, to tenderly recall the good qualities of _____. There was so much that was lovable, beautiful, commendable and genuine in this teenager. [Enlarge if you wish.]

We do not know all the factors regarding his death; it is not our responsibility to know or to speculate. We do know that death has brought release and rest from his distress and suffering.

It is not my prerogative or yours to pronounce ecclesiastical judgments, or promise divine favors; to renounce or eulogize; to censure or reward. These are God's prerogatives alone. Only He understands all from beginning to end; only He knows the influences, failures, and subtleties in life and death.

It is our privilege to love, to cherish, and to remember him and his family. ". . . Love one another," said Jesus, "as I have loved you . . ." (John 15:12).

Paul admonished, think about these things, ". . . whatever is true, whatever is honorable, whatever is just, whatever is pure, whatever is lovely, whatever is gracious, if there is any excellence, if there is anything worthy of praise . . ." (Philippians 4:8 RSV).

We can demonstrate the love of God to _____'s family with our steadfast support and sympathy. What a profound loss it is to them. Friends, form a protective shield that warms and comforts. If there was ever an occasion for you to demonstrate that you care, have concern, and sincerely love, it is now.

There keeps ringing in my mind a song that was popular

some years ago and is relevant now, "Everybody Loves Somebody Sometime." Now is the time for love!

Then
And someday I won't be tired
Not ever, any more,
Someday I'll be calm and free
And walk by the seashore;
It'll all be over
The thing will be done—
The fight will be won or lost.
Then shall I see more clearly
Then shall I really know,
How you have always loved me;
How you have always been here
Standing by my side.
I'll see how I needn't have worried
And tossed and turned about so,
I'll see that it all had a purpose
A way that it had to go;
I'll see that there was direction
Though at times I didn't think so—
And I'll be quiet.[3]

That time is now!

Benediction

... To him who loves us and has freed us from our
sins by his blood and made us a kingdom, priests to
his God and Father, to him be glory and dominion
for ever and ever. Amen.

Revelation 1:5, 6 RSV

Postlude

"O Love That Wilt Not Let Me Go"
"Now the Day Is Over"

3

FOR A SUICIDE

Prelude

"O Holy Spirit, Comforter"
"Jesus, Lover of My Soul"

Opening Sentences

We come to this place as a thirsty land crying out for rain, as a hungry heart seeking for love, as a lonely, frightened sheep in the wilderness, pleading for rescue by the Good Shepherd, as that same sheep nestled in the arms of his rescuer.

We hear the voice of our Father, "Come to me, all who are weary, and hurting and heavy in heart; I will give you peace and healing."[1]

Invocation

O God, the uncreated One, You are present in all places, not in just one place; You are alive in all times, not in just one time; in this chapel and in this hour, we lift up our thoughts beyond all time and all space, to rest in Your everlastingness, to be strengthened by Your presence, there to find hope, through Jesus Christ, our Lord. Amen.

Hymn (optional)

"O Love That Wilt Not Let Me Go"
"The Lord Is My Shepherd"

Old Testament Scripture Readings

General Selections:
Psalm 23
Psalms 46:1, 2, 11

Specifically Relevant Selections:

O Lord, thou hast searched me, and known me.
Thou knowest my downsitting and mine uprising,
thou understandest my thought afar off. . . . Whither
shall I go from thy spirit? or whither shall I flee from
thy presence? If I ascend up into heaven, thou art
there: if I make my bed in hell, behold, thou art there.
If I take the wings of the morning, and dwell in the
uttermost parts of the sea; Even there shall thy hand
lead me, and thy right hand shall hold me. If I say,
Surely the darkness shall cover me; even the night
shall be light about me. Yea, the darkness hideth not
from thee. . . .

Psalms 139:1, 2, 7–12

I call to you, Lord; help me now! Listen to me
when I call to you. Receive my prayer as incense, my
uplifted hands as an evening sacrifice.

Psalms 141:1, 2 TEV

From the depths of my despair I call to you, Lord.
Hear my cry, O Lord; listen to my call for help! . . . I
wait eagerly for the Lord's help, and in his word I
trust. I wait for the Lord more eagerly than watch-
men wait for the dawn. . . . Israel, trust in the Lord,
because his love is constant and he is always willing
to save.

Psalms 130: 1, 2, 5–7 TEV

Let my cry for help reach you, Lord! Give me understanding, as you have promised. Listen to my
prayer, and save me according to your promise! . . .
How I long for your saving help, O Lord! I find happiness in your law. Give me life, so that I may praise
you; may your instructions help me. I wander about
like a lost sheep; so come and look for me, your servant, because I have not neglected your laws.

Psalms 119:169, 170, 174–176 TEV

New Testament Scripture Readings

General Selection:
  1 John 4:7–13

Specifically Relevant Selections:

When Jesus saw the vast crowds he went up the hill-side and after he had sat down his disciples came to him.

Then he began his teaching by saying to them,

"How happy are those who know their need for God, for the kingdom of Heaven is theirs!

"How happy are those who know what sorrow means, for they will be given courage and comfort!

"Happy are those who claim nothing, for the whole earth will belong to them!

"Happy are those who are hungry and thirsty for true goodness, for they will be fully satisfied!

"Happy are the merciful, for they will have mercy shown to them!

"Happy are the utterly sincere, for they will see God!

"Happy are those who make peace, for they will be known as sons of God!

"Happy are those who have suffered persecution for the cause of goodness, for the kingdom of Heaven is theirs!

"And what happiness will be yours when people blame you and ill-treat you and say all kinds of slanderous things against you for my sake! Be glad then, yes, be tremendously glad—for your reward in Heaven is magnificent. They persecuted the prophets before your time in exactly the same way."

Matthew 5:1–12 PHILLIPS

Since therefore we have a great high priest who has passed through the heavens, Jesus the Son of God, let us hold fast to the religion we profess. For ours is not a high priest unable to sympathize with our weak-

nesses, but one who, because of his likeness to us, has
been tested every way, only without sin. Let us therefore boldly approach the throne of our gracious God,
where we may receive mercy and in his grace find
timely help.

Hebrews 4:14–16 NEB

Unison Lord's Prayer

Hymn (optional)

"There Is a Balm in Gilead"

Meditation

A TIME FOR MERCY

A friend of mine told me about a loved one of hers who terminated his life. It was such a devastating shock. He was so
loved; he was an influential person.

At the funeral, only music and Scripture were used. Nothing
personal was said by the minister. Just before the service was to
end, however, a daughter got up and said, "May I say something?" It was rather a strange request, yet she could not cour-
teously be denied. So to his family and friends gathered there
she said, "My dad was a good man. He influenced all of us here
in positive, constructive ways, and we should never forget it.
True, he had periods of depression when he was terribly blue
and down and lost the zest for life. Apparently it was such a
mental state that led to his death. I want you all to remember
his good qualities. We pray for your understanding and God's
mercy upon his loss of emotional control that ended his life.
But remember, please, he was a good man."

What a glorious mastery of the occasion! She saved it from
being a cold, mournful experience.

So we come today to express personal appreciation for the
life and the contribution of our friend, _____. We are all
loved ones of _____. Let us recall the good qualities and

deeds, keeping them foremost in our minds. [Enlarge on the personal life.]

We also come to express condolence and to be merciful to those upon whom this tragedy has fallen. Jesus commended the merciful. This is an appropriate time for mercy.

Mercy is concern for people in misery. It means helping those who hurt, those who suffer the distressing blows of adversity.

There is a helpful book written by Charles R. Swindoll, entitled *Improving Your Serve.* All of us need to become better comforters. Mercy is not just sympathy or simply feeling sorry for someone. Mercy is the ability to get on the inside of another person's skin.

It is a deliberate effort of the mind and the will to so identify with the sorrowing person that we see things as he sees them and feel things as he feels them. Rather than watching from a distance, or keeping detached at arm's length, the merciful get involved, get in touch, offer assistance that alleviates pain. They give more than pious words; they reduce the misery.

Dear sorrowing friends, we promise to render to you a ministry of mercy.

That Most Difficult Thing
That most difficult thing—
To see something
From someone else's point of view.

To let go of ourselves enough
To be able to care,
To let go enough
To be aware,
To let go enough
To sit still and listen
Intently—
Taking it all in. . . .

To get inside someone else's skin
And feel what they feel,
Their joy, their sorrow
As though it were our own—
To know.[2]

A woman testified that when she lost a loved one, she was so overwhelmed with grief that she did not function well at all. Help came her way, she said, in the form of a little lady who visited her every day, ostensibly to help with the work. This lady had only a third-grade education. But she had lost a child and had spent a lifetime with her hand in God's hand. "She saw beneath the surface to my tortured soul," said this woman, "and she comforted me with the comfort she had learned from God. She started me on the road to healing."

"Blessed are the merciful, for they shall obtain mercy."

If we do not do so effectively, we commend to you Jesus Christ, our Lord, who communicates the love of God, the Holy Comforter. God, by becoming human, got right inside our skin, literally. That made it possible for Him to see life through our human eyes, to feel the sting of pain, and to identify with human agony. So God understands your feelings.

Jesus, the Son of God, is our High Priest. He has gone to heaven itself to help us. Therefore, never stop trusting Him. He understands. He faced the same sorrows, frustrations, hurting, and temptations that we do—yet He never gave way. ". . . In the world you have tribulation; but be of good cheer, I have overcome the world," said Jesus (John 16:33 RSV). He leaves with us His Holy Spirit, who will comfort you.

Benediction

> Create a pure heart in me, O God, and put a new and loyal spirit in me. . . . Give me again the joy that comes from your salvation, and make me willing to obey you.
>
> Psalms 51:10, 12 TEV

Postlude

"Guide Me, O Thou Great Jehovah"
"Great Is Thy Faithfulness"

4

FOR AN ABUSED CHILD

Prelude

"Angel Voices, Ever Singing"
"Around the Throne of God in Heaven"
"Jesus Loves Me, This I Know"

Sentences of Worship

Jesus is called the Good Shepherd. Isaiah assures us, "He will feed his flock like a shepherd, he will gather the lambs in his arms, he will carry them in his bosom . . ." (Isaiah 40:11 RSV). A good shepherd knows his sheep by name. What a comforting scene to picture today—this child in the loving, protecting arms of Jesus. He is safe in the arms of Jesus; safe on His gentle breast.

Invocation

Dear God, thank You for the merciful provisions for this child, of a home of goodness and love, of security and shelter, removed from peril and pain, that no eye has seen, nor ear heard, nor man conceived, but promised by our loving Lord and believed in by faith. Internalize and deepen in us that assurance, through Jesus Christ our Lord. Amen.

Old Testament Scripture Readings

General Selection:
Psalm 23

Specifically Relevant Selections:

So she went and came unto the man of God to mount Carmel. And it came to pass, when the man of God saw her afar off, that he said to Gehazi his servant, Behold, yonder is that Shunammite. Run now, I pray thee, to meet her, and say unto her, Is it well with thee? is it well with thy husband? is it well with the child? And she answered, It is well.

2 Kings 4:25, 26

Lo, children are an heritage of the Lord: and the fruit of the womb is his reward. As arrows are in the hand of a mighty man; so are children of the youth. Happy is the man that hath his quiver full of them: they shall not be ashamed, but they shall speak with the enemies in the gate.

Psalms 127:3–5

New Testament Scripture Readings

Specifically Relevant Selections:

And they brought young children to him, that he should touch them; and his disciples rebuked those that brought them. But when Jesus saw it, he was much displeased, and said unto them, Suffer the little children to come unto me, and forbid them not: for of such is the kingdom of God. Verily I say unto you, Whosoever shall not receive the kingdom of God as a little child, he shall not enter therein. And he took them up in his arms, put his hands upon them, and blessed them.

Mark 10:13–16

At the same time came the disciples unto Jesus, saying, Who is the greatest in the kingdom of heaven?

And Jesus called a little child unto him, and set him in the midst of them, And said, Verily I say unto you, Except ye be converted, and become as little children, ye shall not enter into the kingdom of heaven. Whosoever therefore shall humble himself as this little child, the same is greatest in the kingdom of heaven. And whoso shall receive one such little child in my name receiveth me. But whoso shall offend one of these little ones which believe in me, it were better for him that a millstone were hanged about his neck, and that he were drowned in the depth of the sea. Woe unto the world because of offences! for it must needs be that offences come; but woe to that man by whom the offence cometh!

Matthew 18:1–7

Ask, and it shall be given you; seek, and ye shall find; knock, and it shall be opened unto you: For every one that asketh receiveth, and he that seeketh findeth; and to him that knocketh it shall be opened. Or what man is there of you, whom if his son ask bread, will he give him a stone? Or if he ask a fish, will he give him a serpent? If ye then, being evil, know how to give good gifts unto your children, how much more shall your Father which is in heaven give good things to them that ask him? Therefore all things whatsoever ye would that men should do to you, do ye even so to them: for this is the law and the prophets. Enter ye in at the strait gate: for wide is the gate, and broad is the way, that leadeth to destruction, and many there be which go in thereat.

Matthew 7:7–13

They shall hunger no more, neither thirst any more; neither shall the sun light on them, nor any heat. For the Lamb which is in the midst of the throne shall feed them, and shall lead them unto living fountains of waters: and God shall wipe away all tears from their eyes.

Revelation 7:16, 17

Hymn (optional)

"Under His Wings"
"I Need Thee Every Hour"

Meditation

LESSONS TO REMEMBER

It is with a whole catalogue of feelings that we have come here today. Feelings of pity, empathy, sadness, anger, hostility, indignation, bitterness, vengeance.

It is a sad day as we commend to God's keeping this child whom He loves so much. "It is not the will of our Heavenly Father that one of these little ones should perish." This child is but one victim in a national epidemic indicative of increased cruelty, disregard for human sanctity, lack of psychological self-control, and spiritual sickness that permeates our society.

Jesus taught two lessons relating to this incident: First is the respect with which God values children, and so should we. Jesus took little children in His arms and said, "of such is the Kingdom of Heaven. . . . unless you turn and become like little children you shall never enter the Kingdom" (*see* Mark 10:15). The qualities of trust, simplicity, innocence, and honesty, characteristic of little children, are tantamount to the qualifications in God's Kingdom. God loves children—all children—and so should we.

Do not fear the future estate of this victim of injustice, "of such is the Kingdom of God."

Also, let us be concerned about the offenders. Jesus implied, "Blessed are those who do the will of God and teach men so, but whoever causes one of these little ones to sin, it will be better for him to have a stone tied around his neck and be drowned in the middle of the sea" (*see* Matthew 18:5, 6).

Those are pretty strong words from the lips of the usually patient, mild Jesus. He had an unusual reverence for the sanctity of children.

We can but pray for God's mercy and forgiveness to remove cruelty within human hearts.

The Bible indicates "a child shall lead them." It is too late for this child to make the contribution to the world for which he was destined. However, if his untimely death calls us to positive action, to cure this kind of treatment to other children, that will be a notable achievement. God works even in such evils as this to bring about some good. So please, dear friends, let this unfortunate death create a new urgency for developing patience, self-control, self-discipline, and reverence for all human beings—beginning with each of you and accomplished in others through Jesus Christ.

> It is no secret
> What God can do.
> What he's done for others
> He'll do for you. . . .[1]

If you let Him!

Pastoral Prayer and Lord's Prayer

Dear God, speak Your word needed by each person here. Quicken us all in conscience.

To Thy merciful and tender care we commit the soul of this dear child, trusting where we do not see, believing what Jesus assured us, and determined to become pure and childlike that we may be fit for reunion in Your presence.

O God, unite us now in worthy attitudes and yearnings as we pray the prayer directed by Jesus our Lord [*unison Lord's Prayer*].

Postlude

"God Be With You Till We Meet Again"

5

FOR A VICTIM OF MURDER

Prelude

"Near to the Heart of God"
"How Great Thou Art"

Opening Sentences

. . . The Lord is the everlasting God, the Creator of the ends of the earth. He does not faint or grow weary, his understanding is unsearchable. He gives power to the faint, and to him who has no might he increases strength.

Isaiah 40:28, 29 RSV

Invocation

O Lord, we cannot cope with this loss of life without Your help. So please, God, put Your hand into our hands, put Your hope into our hopelessness, put Your strength into our weakness, put Your thoughts into our confused minds, put Your Spirit into our hearts. Then we will be able to cope, through Jesus Christ. Amen.

Hymn (optional)

"Cast Thy Burden"
"I Know That My Redeemer Lives"

Old Testament Scripture Readings

General Selections:
Psalms 55:22
Psalms 90:1–6, 10, 12

Specifically Relevant Selections:

> And moreover I saw under the sun the place of judgment, that wickedness was there; and the place of righteousness, that iniquity was there. I said in mine heart, God shall judge the righteous and the wicked: for there is a time there for every purpose and for every work.
>
> Ecclesiastes 3:16, 17

> Remembering mine affliction and my misery, the wormwood and the gall. My soul hath them still in remembrance, and is humbled in me. This I recall to my mind, therefore have I hope. It is of the Lord's mercies that we are not consumed, because his compassions fail not. They are new every morning: great is thy faithfulness. The Lord is my portion, saith my soul; therefore will I hope in him.
>
> Lamentations 3:19–24

New Testament Scripture Readings

General Selections:
2 Corinthians 1:3, 4
Romans 8:35, 37–39

Specifically Relevant Selections:

> Finally, be ye all of one mind, having compassion one of another, love as brethren, be pitiful, be courteous: Not rendering evil for evil, or railing for railing: but contrariwise blessing; knowing that ye are thereunto called, that ye should inherit a blessing.
>
> 1 Peter 3:8, 9

> And there were also two other, malefactors, led with him to be put to death. And when they were come to the place, which is called Calvary, there they crucified him, and the malefactors, one on the right hand, and the other on the left. Then said Jesus, Fa-

ther, forgive them; for they know not what they
do. . . .

                                            Luke 23:32–34

We are troubled on every side, yet not distressed;
we are perplexed, but not in despair; Persecuted, but
not forsaken; cast down, but not destroyed.

                                            2 Corinthians 4:8, 9

Dearly beloved, avenge not yourselves, but rather
give place unto wrath: for it is written, Vengeance is
mine; I will repay, saith the Lord. Therefore if thine
enemy hunger, feed him; if he thirst, give him drink:
for in so doing thou shalt heap coals of fire on his
head.

                                            Romans 12:19, 20

Pastoral Prayer

Gracious God and Father: We come here to pray for our
friends who have sustained this terrible loss. Use the Scriptures
read, the words said, and the prayers lifted up today to sustain
their faith and to bring them comfort. May your Holy Spirit
work with and in them to save them from despair, hostility,
and loss of faith.

We remember with fondness and appreciation the life so
suddenly snatched away. Help the loved ones to concentrate
upon the years of joy, to see the stars and not the darkness.

May the assurance of resurrection and eternal life add another incentive to the good life, in Jesus Christ. Amen.

Hymn (optional)

"Precious Lord, Take My Hand"

Meditation

LESSONS FROM THE CROSS

We come here to express our admiration for _____. Those
who knew this person are deeply grieved with his untimely

death. It cut short a life that meant so much to so many, was so rich in good works, and gave such promise of so much more. [Enlarge here if you wish.]

We never know what a day may bring of sadness or of joy. We all are terribly shocked by the suddenness of this happening. We convey our sense of loss to his dear family, who have been so brave.

Only the assurance that nothing shall separate him from the love of Christ consoles us; not distress, not peril, not sword, nothing in life or death is able to keep him from the love of God. We commend him to God's keeping, cherishing in our own hearts his memory.

The cross of Christ makes two facts plain to us: First, in this world, even the innocent are not exempt from unjust treatment; second, there is a Power that makes us able to rise above tragedy, to find comfort in the face of death. In the cross we see God suffering with us; we see His forgiveness. Through that cross God puts love in us so that we can love; He puts forgiveness in our spirits so we are not bitter and can forgive those who have done us injustice. Jesus shows us how to meet suffering, ". . . In the world you have tribulation; but be of good cheer, I have overcome the world" (John 16:33 RSV).

On the evening of April 25, 1958, a young Korean exchange student at the University of Pennsylvania left the dormitory room to mail a letter to his parents in Pusan, Korea. As he turned from the mailbox drop at the corner of the campus, six leather-jacketed teenage boys began assaulting him. They used clubs, sticks, rocks. They kicked him and finally hit him over the head with a lead pipe. When they finished their crime, they vanished, and the boy was dead, much to the consternation and shock of the entire community. The six boys were apprehended and the district attorney secured legal authority to try the boys for the death penalty.

The parents of the victim were consumed in grief, disillusionment, and anger. However, after months of working through their feelings, they wrote the judge, saying,

"Our family has met together and we have decided to petition that the most generous treatment possible within the laws of your government be given to those who have committed this criminal action. In order to give evidence of our sincere hope contained in this petition, we have decided to save money to start a fund to be used for the religious, educational and vocational and social guidance of the boys when they are released. We have dared to express our hope with a spirit received from the Gospel of our Savior, Jesus Christ who died for our sins."

What a spirit!

It is like the perfume that a flower gives when it is stepped on by a heel. Can you find this spirit in your heart? It will save you from resentment and bitterness and will instead give you both gratitude for the life that was and an identification with Jesus, who was vindicated with resurrection.

Benediction

> I'm all right now
> Thank you, Father,
> I can feel the rock
> Under my feet again.[1]

Postlude

"In the Cross of Christ I Glory"
"God Will Take Care of You"

6

FOR A MURDERER

Prelude

"Dear Lord and Father of Mankind"

Sentences of Worship

> O Lord, thou hast searched me, and known me.
> Thou knowest my downsitting and mine uprising,

thou understandest my thought afar off. Thou compassest my path and my lying down, and art acquainted with all my ways. For there is not a word in my tongue, but, lo, O Lord, thou knowest it altogether. Thou hast beset me behind and before, and laid thine hand upon me. Such knowledge is too wonderful for me; it is high, I cannot attain unto it.

Psalms 139:1–6

Invocation

All-knowing God, unto whom all hearts are open, all desires known, and from whom no secrets are hid, we come in contrition and humility, seeking a sense of Thy mercy and forgiveness upon our foolish ways and a cleansing of the thoughts of our minds, so that we may come to love Thee more perfectly and follow Thee more faithfully and to trust Thy ways more sincerely, through Jesus Christ, the Lord. Amen.

Hymn (optional)

"From Every Stormy Wind That Blows," verses 1, 4

Old Testament Scripture Readings

General Selections:
   Psalms 103:11, 13, 14
   Psalms 39:5, 7, 8, 12, 13
   Isaiah 54:8, 10

Specifically Relevant Selections:

Surely thou wilt slay the wicked, O God: depart from me therefore, ye bloody men. For they speak against thee wickedly, and thine enemies take thy name in vain. Do not I hate them, O Lord, that hate thee? and am not I grieved with those that rise up against thee? I hate them with perfect hatred: I count them mine enemies. Search me, O God, and know my heart: try me, and know my thoughts: And see if there be any wicked way in me, and lead me in the way everlasting.

Psalms 139:19–24

But he, being full of compassion, forgave their iniquity, and destroyed them not: yea, many a time turned he his anger away, and did not stir up all his wrath. For he remembered that they were but flesh; a wind that passeth away, and cometh not again.

Psalms 78:38, 39

New Testament Scripture Readings

General Selection:
  John 14:27

Specifically Relevant Selection:

My little children, these things write I unto you, that ye sin not. And if any man sin, we have an advocate with the Father, Jesus Christ the righteous: And he is the propitiation for our sins: and not for ours only, but also for the sins of the whole world. And hereby we do know that we know him, if we keep his commandments. . . . Brethren, I write no new commandment unto you, but an old commandment which ye had from the beginning. . . . He that saith he is in the light, and hateth his brother, is in darkness even until now. He that loveth his brother abideth in the light. . . . But he that hateth his brother is in darkness, and walketh in darkness, and knoweth not whither he goeth, because that darkness hath blinded his eyes. . . . Love not the world, neither the things that are in the world. If any man love the world, the love of the Father is not in him. For all that is in the world, the lust of the flesh, and the lust of the eyes, and the pride of life, is not of the Father, but is of the world. And the world passeth away, and the lust thereof: but he that doeth the will of God abideth for ever.

1 John 2:1–3, 7, 9–11, 15–17

Meditation

ENEMIES ARE HUMAN, TOO

Our text is the words of Jesus, "Love your enemies and pray for those who persecute you, so that you may be sons of your Father who is in heaven . . ." (Matthew 5:44 RSV).

Our sensibilities have been tested by this man's evil actions.

He has committed crime against so many innocent victims.

He has broken God's agelong law for cooperate living, "Thou shalt not kill."

He has jarred the conscience of human justice. He has brought embarrassment, heartache, worry, and understandable regret to his family. To them we convey our deepest sorrow.

In no way can we condone what he has done or take away personal responsibility.

The Bible is clear, ". . . The soul that sins shall die" (Ezekiel 18:4 RSV). "The wages of sin is death . . ." (Romans 6:23). Our society has tolerated so much that is intolerable to God that we have blurred right and wrong, protected the offender rather than the victims and reversed our values.

I suppose if we knew the total background of this man's life and the influences that molded and formulated his character, we might see where society and others share some of the responsibility.

Only God knows all, so He alone can be the all righteous judge. That is why the Bible quotes, "Vengeance is mine," says the Lord, "I will repay" (*see* Romans 12:19).

Though our initial inclination is one of vengeance, yet such must be reserved for a wisdom greater than our own.

This has not been easily achieved. In the ancient civilizations, prior to the time of Moses, retaliation was total. Entire clans or nations might be wiped out to pay for the crimes of a few.

Moses made a great step in limiting vengeance. He said "an eye for an eye, and a tooth for a tooth," meaning that if someone kills one of yours, you can kill one of his, but no more.

Later the prophets said there should be no retaliation. "Vengeance belongs only to God; he will repay."

When Jesus came, He eliminated the entire business of retaliation by saying, ". . . Love your enemies and pray for those who persecute you . . ." (Matthew 5:44 RSV). ". . . overcome evil with good" (Romans 12:21 RSV). Convert the sinner, do not destroy him. Remember, enemies are human, too.

For his own persecutors, Jesus prayed, "Father, forgive them; for they know not what they do" (Luke 23:34 RSV). Following our Lord's example, then, we pray for this one who has brought human suffering. We allow God's judgment to prevail. We will not take His judgment into our own hands. There is no total justice upon the earth, not as long as innocent people are killed by savage men. In God's future, we are confident the injustice will be righted; evil will be punished and the good will be vindicated and rewarded.

Pastoral Prayer

Lord, we are glad the responsibility is not ours to deal with human destiny.

According to Your knowledge and mercy is the future determination. We trust You; so wipe from our minds the nightmare. Mellow our angered spirits, feed our souls so that we may transcend our embarrassment, shame, and bitterness. Help us to live in Your Spirit.

Dear God, comfort with Your love the family and loved one of this person. Surround them with compassionate friends who understand and who stick "closer than a brother." Help them to assimilate the loss, to find forgiveness, and to build their tomorrows in Your will.

Help us all to teach and to witness to the truth of Jesus Christ, so that men shall study war no more and shall convert the implements of destruction into human betterment. Busy our efforts in changing human beings, for changed people change the world—not by might, nor by power, but by Thy Spirit, O Lord of Hosts. So may it be. Amen.

Postlude

"Lead, Kindly Light"

7

FOR A POLICEMAN KILLED ON DUTY

Prelude

"In the Hour of Trial"
"My Faith Looks Up to Thee"

Opening Sentences

The Lord is my light and my salvation; whom shall I fear? the Lord is the strength of my life; of whom shall I be afraid?

Psalms 27:1

Invocation

Our God and our Father, whose love is everlasting and whose mercy knows no limits; help us now to turn to You with reverent spirits and believing minds, so that we may think Your thoughts after You, hear the words of Scripture whereby we may find hope, and be lifted out of our darkness in the light of Jesus Christ, and may find peace and comfort in Your Holy Presence, in Jesus' name. Amen.

Hymn (optional)

"The Old Rugged Cross"
"Beneath the Cross of Jesus"

Old Testament Scripture Reading

General Selections:
Psalm 130
2 Samuel 22:2, 3

39

Specifically Relevant Selections:

> What time I am afraid, I will trust in thee. In God I will praise his word, in God I have put my trust; I will not fear what flesh can do unto me.
>
> Psalms 56:3, 4

> And he said, The Lord is my rock, and my fortress, and my deliverer; The God of my rock; in him will I trust: he is my shield, and the horn of my salvation, my high tower, and my refuge, my saviour; thou savest me from violence.
>
> 2 Samuel 22:2, 3

New Testament Scripture Readings

General Selection:
  1 Peter 1:3–9

Specifically Relevant Selections:

> Lay not up for yourselves treasures upon earth, where moth and rust doth corrupt, and where thieves break through and steal: But lay up for yourselves treasures in heaven, where neither moth nor rust doth corrupt, and where thieves do not break through nor steal: For where your treasure is, there will your heart be also.
>
> Matthew 6:19–21

> And he said unto them, Take heed, and beware of covetousness: for a man's life consisteth not in the abundance of the things which he possesseth.
>
> Luke 12:15

> For one is approved if, mindful of God, he endures pain while suffering unjustly. For what credit is it, if when you do wrong and are beaten for it you take it patiently? But if when you do right and suffer for it you take it patiently, you have God's approval. For to this you have been called, because Christ also suf-

fered for you, leaving you an example, that you should follow in his steps. He committed no sin; no guile was found on his lips. When he was reviled, he did not revile in return; when he suffered, he did not threaten; but he trusted to him who judges justly. He himself bore our sins in his body on the tree, that we might die to sin and live to righteousness. By his wounds you have been healed. For you were straying like sheep, but have now returned to the Shepherd and Guardian of your souls.

1 Peter 2:19–25 RSV

Finally, be ye all of one mind, having compassion one of another, love as brethren, be pitiful, be courteous: Not rendering evil for evil, or railing for railing: but contrariwise blessing; knowing that ye are thereunto called, that ye should inherit a blessing.

1 Peter 3:8, 9

Poem

Well Done

Servant of God, well done!
 Rest from thy loved employ;
The battle fought, the victory won,
 Enter thy Master's joy.
The pains of death are past,
 Labour and sorrow cease.
And life's long warfare closed at last,
 Thy soul is found in peace.[1]

Pastoral Prayer

Almighty God, our heavenly Father, in whose wisdom and mercy is the future; have mercy upon us as we draw near to You.

We are grateful for the life and service of our friend and for those qualities that endeared him to so many.

Dear God, look with tender mercy upon these beloved friends. Enable them to find strength and comfort. Deliver them, we pray, from bitterness and despair. Fill their hearts with peace.

Speak to us of Thy forgiving love, O God. You have taught us to love You with all our hearts, minds, souls, and strength and our neighbors as ourself. How far we have fallen short. We plead Your forgiveness, remembering the comforting words of Jesus, "Whoever comes to me, I will not cast out" (*see* John 6:37).

Now that our hearts are opened and our spirits quickened, speak to us of eternal matters so that we may hear and obey Jesus Christ. Amen.

Meditation

THE SECRET OF SECURITY

We are here to join this family in honoring the memory and service of _____, one of our public servants. As a grateful community we say, "Thank you for a job fruitfully done. No greater love has any man than this, that a man lay down his life for the protection and welfare of his friends." _____ had worked as a policeman for many years. He had risked his life on countless occasions, as does every law-enforcement officer. Regretfully he was killed while on duty. We convey our profoundest sorrow to his nearest and dearest. We are proud of him and you for your mutual sacrifices for the public welfare.

We need to show our appreciation for these who protect us. They need greater public support for what they do. Let us do everything in our power to respect their authority, to rewin for them legal support in carrying out their duties, and to counter those disrespectful elements in our community.

Why would anyone be a policeman? Of course, someone has to protect our citizens and maintain community order and enforce the law. Yet it is so dangerous. Crime is getting out of hand. Wouldn't one always be afraid? What kept this man, and is keeping others, from fear?

May I suggest a basic faith to dispel our fears in whatever we face in life?

Jesus once said, in essence, "Do not fear them that can destroy the body only . . . rather fear him who can destroy both the body and the soul in hell" (*see* Matthew 10:28). There is one thing worse than dying physically; and that is dying spiritually. The forces to fear most are the insidious influences that plague the spirit of man even more than those that kill the body.

A friend tells about sitting at his dining-room window one afternoon during a violent summer thunderstorm. A few feet away stood a weeping willow tree, tossed and rolled by the strong winds. Suddenly he leaped to his feet. On one of those tossing branches was a bird singing at the top of his voice. My friend's first impulse was to say, "You fool bird! Why should you be singing at a time like this? Don't you know the limb may break and go crashing at any instant?" Then it dawned on him the secret of the bird's security. He related it in the words: "On the bough that swings there's a bird that sings, because he knows he's got wings."[2] The bird could face the threatening storm and sing because he had wings.

Paul, the Apostle, wrote from a cold, dirty, prison dungeon, "I consider that the sufferings of this present time are not worth comparing with the glory that is to be revealed to us" (Romans 8:18 RSV).

When you know that man is more than a body and life continues even after the body is killed—then you can find stability, peace, and security even in terrifying times and in dangerous jobs, like these policemen, because we have wings!

Benediction

"The grace of the Lord Jesus Christ and the love of God and the fellowship of the Holy Spirit be with you all" (2 Corinthians 13:14 RSV). Amen.

Postlude

"Now the Day Is Over"

8

FOR A MISSING PERSON FOUND WITH BODY DECOMPOSED

Prelude

"The Strife Is O'er"

Opening Sentences

With sensitive hearts we come here in reverence, appreciation, and wonder. We enter into fellowship with God the Eternal Being, to think His thoughts, to feel His feelings, and to commune soul with soul.

"Cast thy burden on the Lord, and he shall sustain thee . . ." (Psalms 55:22).

Invocation

Our Father and God, we bow before You. We are not asking for special favors as though You were a Celestial Santa Claus. We are not asking for escape from the liabilities of being human. We don't want anything heroic or to bargain with You; we just want to be able to bear with courage and maturity the things we have to face. Help us to do it, we pray, in Jesus' name. Amen.

Hymn (optional)

"My Faith Looks Up to Thee"

Old Testament Scripture Readings

General Selections:
  Psalms 55:22
  Psalms 139:7–10

Specifically Relevant Selection:

> Remember the word unto thy servant, upon which thou hast caused me to hope. This is my comfort in my affliction: for thy word hath quickened me. The proud have had me greatly in derision: yet have I not declined from thy law. I remembered thy judgments of old, O Lord; and have comforted myself. Horror hath taken hold upon me because of the wicked that forsake thy law. Thy statutes have been my songs in the house of my pilgrimage. I have remembered thy name, O Lord, in the night, and have kept thy law. This I had, because I kept thy precepts.
>
> Psalms 119:49–56

New Testament Scripture Readings

General Selection:
1 Corinthians 15:53–58

Specifically Relevant Selection:

> We are troubled on every side, yet not distressed; we are perplexed, but not in despair; Persecuted, but not forsaken; cast down, but not destroyed; Always bearing about in the body the dying of the Lord Jesus, that the life also of Jesus might be made manifest in our body. For we which live are always delivered unto death for Jesus' sake, that the life also of Jesus might be made manifest in our mortal flesh. So then death worketh in us, but life in you. We having the same spirit of faith, according as it is written, I believed, and therefore have I spoken; we also believe, and therefore speak; Knowing that he which raised up the Lord Jesus shall raise up us also by Jesus, and shall present us with you. For all things are for your sakes, that the abundant grace might through the thanksgiving of many redound to the glory of God.
>
> 2 Corinthians 4:8–15

Pastoral Prayer

Father God, the parent and comforter of Your children—we pray for Your sustaining grace to support these who mourn at this time.

We thank You for the life of _____, whose qualities of character and personal relationships have endeared him to those of us gathered here—and especially to his family.

We are grateful, our Father, for the assurance in Jesus that death is not the destruction but the expansion of life; that it opens the way to new realms with new opportunities of growth and service; that death does not take us away from Your fatherly care, nor separate us from Your love. We do not know the details, for we cannot see, but we are assured by the eyes of faith that we never leave Your presence. We are children of Your love, and underneath are the everlasting arms. So even amid our distress, affirm our faith, love, and hope so that we may know the peace that passes all understanding, in Jesus' name. Amen.

Meditation

A BUILDING FROM GOD

For months we have been perplexed. For months we had hoped it wasn't so. For months we have suffered with this family.

Now we know. The mystery has come to light. The sad ordeal is over. The body has been found. Our hopes for survival have vanished.

We come here to empathize and weep with this family, to convey our understanding and to try to bring the comfort of faith, hope, and love. We cast our burdens upon the Lord, whose wisdom and mercy are from everlasting to everlasting.

We all will remember this beautiful person who enjoyed life so very much, who had so many friends and accomplished so much in life. Our hearts ache for his family in facing the unknown ordeal, and our spirits reach out to these dear neighbors.

In the Bible is a very familiar verse which we all have heard, but which takes on particular significant meaning today, ". . . If the earthly house of our tabernacle be dissolved, we have a building from God, a house not made with hands, eternal in the heavens" (*see* 2 Corinthians 5:1).

Occasionally, as a minister, I hear people say, "I can't stand to leave my loved one out there in the cemetery," or, "I can't bear the thought of the body decomposing." We who are Christians do not believe our loved ones are in the cemetery or in the casket. We leave only their earthly house, or as someone has said, "their wornout suit." To believing Christians, a cemetery is the emptiest place in the world—nobody is there. It is only the physical remains left behind. For the real person, the journey lies ahead in the spiritual world where God resides.

When the grand old man John Quincy Adams turned fourscore, while hobbling down the street one day in Boston, he was asked, "How is John Quincy Adams this morning?" The old man turned slowly and said, "Fine, son, fine. The old house that John Quincy has been living in is not so good. The underpinning is about to go. The thatch is gone on the roof. The windows are so dim John Quincy can hardly see anymore. It wouldn't surprise me if before the winter is over, he had to move out. But as for John Quincy Adams, he never was better—never was better."

The real John Quincy Adams was a soul, a spirit, a personality. For him death was only a "moving day." The old earthly house in which he had lived so long would return to the dust. Death would come as a friend to release him from worry, fear, and suffering. ". . . There shall be no more crying, nor sorrow . . . neither shall there be any more pain . . ." (*see* Revelation 21:4). Though the outward body decay, we are renewed inwardly day by day.

We all will face death sooner or later. May we be like the gentleman whose health was fading and whose loved ones had preceded him. He said to his pastor, "Well, I've got a few things I need to do to get ready. There is one favor I would like to ask of you, pastor. Help me not to lose this point of view, so I can walk straight into the sunset with my head up."

Benediction

"If I take the wings of the morning, and dwell in the utter-most parts of the sea; Even there shall thy hand lead me, and thy right hand shall hold me" (Psalms 139:9, 10). Send us forth, O Lord, with this abiding assurance. Amen.

Postlude

"Nearer My God to Thee"
"Blest Be the Tie"

9

FOR AN INFANT CRIB DEATH

Prelude

"Come Unto Me, Ye Weary"

Opening Sentence

The Spirit of the Lord God is upon me; because the Lord hath anointed me to preach good tidings unto the meek; he hath sent me to bind up the broken-hearted . . . to comfort all that mourn . . . to give unto them beauty for ashes, the oil of joy for mourning, the garment of praise for the spirit of heaviness; that they might be called trees of righteousness. . . .

Isaiah 61:1–3

Invocation

O God of peace and love, who has taught us that in quiet-ness and confidence shall be our strength, in faith and love shall be our refuge, by the might of Thy Spirit, lift us, we pray, into Thy Presence, where we may be still and know that Thou art God and that all is well with the soul of the child; through Jesus Christ our Lord. Amen.

Hymn (optional)

"The King of Love My Shepherd Is"

Old Testament Scripture Reading

General Selections:
Psalm 23
2 Kings 4:25, 26

New Testament Scripture Readings

General Selection:
Mark 10:13–16

Specifically Relevant Selections:

... When we cry, "Abba! Father!" it is the Spirit himself bearing witness with our spirit that we are children of God, and if children, then heirs, heirs of God and fellow heirs with Christ, provided we suffer with him in order that we may also be glorified with him.

Romans 8:15–17 RSV

These things I have spoken unto you, that in me ye might have peace. In the world ye shall have tribulation: but be of good cheer; I have overcome the world.

John 16:33

Prayer

O God of love and mercy, You know better than we the anguish of these parents whose joy has been turned into sorrow and whose home has been left desolate by this unexplainable and sudden loss. Since You suffered the loss of Your own special Son, we feel, Lord, that you understand the pain and sorrow of these dear friends.

O Lord, by Your Holy Spirit free them from bitterness and

self-recrimination. Help them to look beyond the darkness of
the night, to the stars, by remembering the joys this child
brought to their hearts. Let faith sustain them in hope and
love. Let the things unseen and eternal grow more real, more
present, more full of meaning. We thank You, O God, for the
assurance that love can never lose its own and that children inherit the Kingdom of heaven. May this certitude add incentive
to the good life and fill your minds with peace, through Jesus
Christ our Lord. Amen.

Hymn (optional)

"Jesus Loves Me"
"He Shall Feed His Flock" from Handel's *Messiah*

Meditation

WHEN FAITH IS DIFFICULT

A park ranger said to visitors at the Grand Canyon, "It is
eight miles down and eighty miles back. However," he continued, "the Grand Canyon is beautiful on a sunny day, when
you can see both the shades and the shadows."

In the journey of life we all will visit the Canyon of Sorrow
and Bereavement. Our dear friends [parents' names] have
plunged suddenly to the canyon's depths with the crib death of
their [name of child]. It has come as a shock for which no one
is ever prepared. There is no logical or medical explanation.
He was such a sweet, healthy baby, the apple of their eye. Be
assured, you parents are not to blame; it was not your fault.
Yet feelings of guilt quite naturally surface. You may be saying, "If I had only done this," or, "If we had only checked." It
is one of the mysterious tragedies, not of your making at all.
"For now we see in a mirror dimly, but then face to face. Now
I know in part; then I shall understand fully . . ." (1 Corinthians 13:12 RSV).

We have come to this place where you can let your tears
overflow. Other emotions of resentment, bitterness, even hos-

tility may build up. They need a vent for expression as well. You will have doubts, become depressed and despondent. It is a part of grief.

None of us can understand completely the feelings you have. We are here to share your loss, to convey our sympathy, to help in every way possible.

Only eight miles to the bottom of Grand Canyon; so rapid did the sorrow come. It is a long, hard way out of the valley, but there is a way out. "Yea, though I walk through the valley of the shadow of death, I will fear no evil: for thou art with me . . ." said the Psalmist (Psalms 23:4).

Listen, dear friends. Here are helpful steps out of the valley of depression.

1. Accept the fact that your baby is dead.
2. Remember, all healing takes time. You cannot absorb this loss in a few days, but the days, months, and years will heal the wounds of your soul.
3. Talk freely about your child, the joy that came to your life. Talking gives sorrow wings; it flies away so you can see the sky and the stars and remember the goodness of the Lord.
4. Get up! Get out! Get going! Do not withdraw. Life goes on.
5. So busy yourself in a purpose.
6. Finally, take your burdens to the Lord and leave them there. Deepen your faith. Think of all the problems he has escaped in this world, and project the joys that must be his in the house God has prepared for children, for "of such is the Kingdom of God."

Benediction

> The Lord bless thee, and keep thee: The Lord make his face shine upon thee, and be gracious unto thee: The Lord lift up his countenance upon thee, and give thee peace.

> Numbers 6:24–26

Postlude

"How Strong and Sweet My Father's Care"

10

FOR THE TRAGIC DEATH OF A CHILD

Prelude

"Lead, Kindly Light"
"Saviour, Like a Shepherd Lead Us"
"The King of Love My Shepherd Is"

Sentences of Worship

"I am the good shepherd. . . ," said Jesus. "My sheep hear my voice, and I know them, and they follow me: And I give unto them eternal life; and they shall never perish, neither shall any man pluck them out of my hand" (John 10:11, 27, 28).

Invocation

Dear God, Father of mercy, giver of all comfort, deal graciously with these who mourn, that casting their burdens upon Thee, they may know the consolation of Thy love, the support of dear and understanding friends, and the assurance of children's entrance into Thine eternal Kingdom. Sustain them in faith, hope, and love, through Jesus Christ, the Lord. Amen.

Hymn (optional)

"The Lord Is My Shepherd"

Old Testament Scripture Readings

General Selections:
Deuteronomy 33:27
Psalms 55:22
Psalms 147:3
2 Samuel 12:16–23
Isaiah 40:1; 41:9, 10, 13

Specifically Relevant Selection:

> ... He shall gather the lambs with his arm, and carry them in his bosom, and shall gently lead those that are with young.
>
> Isaiah 40:11

New Testament Scripture Readings

General Selections:
Matthew 18:1–5, 10
Mark 10:13–16

Specifically Relevant Selections:

> Blessed are the pure in heart: for they shall see God.
>
> Matthew 5:8

> Blessed are they that mourn: for they shall be comforted.
>
> Matthew 5:4

Pastoral Prayer

Our Heavenly Parent, who knows and cares for each of us; we thank Thee for the eternal home of joy and love where little children play and sing and grow, amid scenes of peace and blessedness.

We are thankful that for a little while at least these good people, our friends, were granted this gift of Thy love, to be for them a sacred memory, lifting their thoughts beyond these sorrowful days, to Thy presence and the abode where the child of their love with Thee awaits their heavenly homecoming. May this memory and this hope remain ever in their hearts and be an incentive to holy devotion.

Dear God, help us all amid the trials and tribulations of our earthly life to keep within us the spirit of little children, knowing that our Lord promised such His favor and blessing. May we strive to remove from this earth everything that would damage little children. Grant us to use our efforts so that children may come into their rightful heritage, developed in the image of the Babe who entered the world, then grew in wisdom and stature and in favor with Thee and all men. So may it be. Amen.

Hymn (optional)

"He Shall Feed His Flock"
"Saviour, Like a Shepherd Lead Us"

Meditation

PICK UP THE PIECES AND MAKE SOMETHING OF THEM

Rabbi Harold S. Kushner, author of the provocative book *When Bad Things Happen to Good People,* records that one day he received a phone call informing him that a five-year-old boy in the neighborhood had run out into the street after a ball, had been hit by a car, and was killed. He did not know the boy; the family was not a part of his congregation. Nonetheless he went to the service.

In the eulogy, the family's clergyman said, "This is not a time for sadness or tears. This is a time for rejoicing, because Michael has been taken out of this world of sin and pain with his innocent soul unstained by sin. He is in a happier land now where there is no pain and no grief; let us thank God for that."[1]

Rabbi Kushner said that he felt so bad for Michael's parents.

Not only had they lost a child without warning, they were being told by a representative of their religion that they should rejoice. Of course they did not feel like rejoicing. They felt hurt; they felt angry; they felt that God had been unfair to them.

Their minister assumed God to be the cause of this tragedy, when in fact God is not behind everything that happens. Some things happen that are not the will of God at all. There is human element in many happenings. Sometimes there are no logical reasons at all for tragic happenings. Such happenings as this betrays all human explanations.

In Psalm 121 we read, "I will lift up mine eyes unto the hills, from whence cometh my help. My help cometh from the Lord, which made heaven and earth" (Psalms 121:1, 2). He does not say, "My tragedy comes from the Lord." He says, "My *help* comes from the Lord." The question to ask is not, "Why has God done this to me?" Rather pray, "O God, help me through this painful ordeal."

You are not being scolded for weeping; indeed you need to weep. Who among us would not weep? We are not denying that "of such is the kingdom of God," and to be sure it helps to assuage the pain and adds incentive to heaven. But please do not blame God for this child's death. Do not escape its pain. Your help in dealing with the anger, hostility, guilt, and resentment is in the Lord. "My help comes from the Lord!"

The dean of Yale Divinity School relates the story of his five-year-old son, who with his mother's help worked weeks to make his father a surprise Christmas gift. It was a beautiful ceramic vase for his office. The vase was carefully decorated with a ribbon, then placed far out of sight under the Christmas tree, to be protected from breakage. The boy was utterly excited about the secret. Finally, when Christmas morning came and the family was gathered about the tree, the boy pulled the vase from behind the tree and joyously took it to his father. As he did so, he stumbled. The vase fell against the rocker and shattered into a hundred pieces. The boy broke down in uncontrollable tears. The father, attempting to console the boy, said, "Son, don't cry. I thank you for the gift, but it's not worth crying about. Don't you worry a thing about it."

The mother, being much wiser than the father, took the boy in her arms. "Of course it was important," she said. "We worked so hard on it!" She cried with her son. Finally, when his tears had subsided, she said, "Son, let's pick up the pieces and make something of them."

So it is all right to cry. It is important to weep. But when your tears subside, you must pick up the pieces and make something of what is left—for life must go on.

May God help you through and after this loss, not to go to pieces, but to pick up the pieces.

Benediction

> The grace of our Lord Jesus Christ,
>   the love of God,
>   and the communion of the Holy
> Spirit be with us all to the end,
>   and in the end. Amen.

Postlude

"God Be With You"
"Still, Still With Thee"

11

FOR A NATURALLY ABORTED BABY

Opening Sentences

What joy this conception brought to you! The news and expectations surely were cherished. A precious life was conceived. Sadly we accept the death. We surrender the soul to God's love and keeping. You, dear friends, have a "family support system," drawn close by this mutual loss. May "faith, hope and love" sustain you through all the days of your life.

Appropriate Scriptures

Psalm 23
Isaiah 40:11
Matthew 5:8
John 14:1–3, 27

Pastoral Prayer

O God, Author of life, whose ways are hidden, yet whose marvelous works are experienced every hour of every day; we share with these parents the loss and disappointment they feel with the premature death of one for whom they had yearned. We commend to Thy keeping this little life, not yet developed, but a soul nonetheless, to be gathered in the garden of souls, to grow in beauty and to dwell forever in Thy presence. Grant to him the fullness of joy and Thy tenderest blessings forever. Breathe Thy peace into every aching heart and support these parents through this experience. May the common loss draw them closer than ever before to one another, to their families, and to Thee, in whom is the eternal reunion of childlike and loving souls, in Jesus Christ. Amen.

Meditation

JUST FOR THIS MOMENT

Dr. Barry Bailey, a well-known minister, relates that years ago he visited in a hospital with a young woman who was about seven months pregnant. Her doctor and his colleagues had told her they could see no way to save her baby. She understood she was going to lose her child. As he was about to leave she said to him, "Dr. Bailey, if I lose my baby I can stand it, because I know it is God's will." Sometimes it is not wise to try to counsel with anyone in such a situation, but somehow that seemed like the proper time to say what he thought she needed to hear, so he said, "If you don't mind, I would like to talk with you about this very honestly for a few moments." She agreed, so he said, "I want to tell you it is not God's will that you lose this baby. If you lose your baby and you are hurt, God is hurt, too. It is as simple as that."

That is as far as he got before she reached out and took his hand. She started to cry and said, "I only said that because I thought I should, to be religious. I wondered how I could believe in a God who would take my baby." He said, "Think of all the advances which have been made in medicine, and think of the things we will be able to do some day that we cannot do now. Does that mean God has changed? God is always on your side. Your baby's death is not the will of God."[1]

"It is not the will of your Father...," said Jesus, "that one of these little ones should perish" (Matthew 18:14). There is no logical or adequate explanation. It is painful. It is one of those unfortunate happenings that has no reason, except that an early abortion probably means something was wrong, and this is nature's way of correction.

Premature twins were born to a certain woman. One of the babies died shortly after birth. The supporting family was at the parents' side as they wept. Before the baby was taken from the room, the family passed it around to be held and loved by each family member. The last to get to hold her was the mother, who through her tears and crying whispered, "I would do this all over again, just for you, my dear, just for this moment with you."

Benediction

May the sustaining power of faith, hope, and love be yours this day and all the days of your life, through Jesus Christ the Lord. Amen.

12

FOR A VICTIM OF CANCER

Prelude Music

"When I Survey the Wondrous Cross"
"For All the Saints Who From Their Labors Rest"

Opening Sentences

"Come unto me, all ye that labour and are heavy laden, and I will give you rest" (Matthew 11:28). "Our help is in the name of the Lord, who made heaven and earth" (Psalms 124:8).

Invocation

O God, Creator of all, in whose nature psychedelic butterflies painfully emerge from the larva and beautiful lilies bloom from dried-out bulbs; how comforting to know beyond the travail of bodily death is the glory of new life, assured by Jesus Christ who said, "Because I live, you too shall live." Blessed be the wisdom and love of God. Amen.

Hymn (optional)

"The Old Rugged Cross"
"Wonderful Peace"

Old Testament Scripture Readings

General Selections:
Psalm 23
Psalms 103:1–4
Ecclesiastes 3:1–8, 10, 11

Specifically Relevant Selection:

> Fear thou not; for I am with thee: be not dismayed;
> for I am thy God: I will strengthen thee; yea, I will
> help thee; yea, I will uphold thee with the right hand
> of my righteousness. . . . For I the Lord thy God will
> hold thy right hand, saying unto thee, Fear not; I will
> help thee.
>
> Isaiah 41:10, 13

New Testament Scripture Readings

General Selections:
  Matthew 11:28–30
  John 14:1–3
  2 Corinthians 4:16–18
  1 Thessalonians 4:13, 14

Hymn (optional)

"Great Is Thy Faithfulness," verses 1, 3

Meditation

JOY UNUTTERABLE

It was only a few months ago that the doctors discovered
that _____ had cancer. This began for her and her family days
of bitter truth and nights of anxious vigil. Two days ago she
exchanged the suffering that she had borne so courageously for
the peace that she so richly deserved. Throughout the ordeal,
she and her family have been reinforced by their Christian
faith, the caring concern of dear friends, and the promise of a
"land beyond the river that we call our sweet forever."

When a dear friend of mine, Kathleen Bailey Austin, died of
cancer, her husband, Spencer, shared with me the testimonies
of her many friends, as well as his own. Let me share excerpts
of these that speak in helpful ways on this occasion:

About her sudden illness it was said, "But Kathleen doesn't
get sick. . . . This is most unbelievable! . . . We were devastated

about the news. She has always been so vibrant and alive. . . . No, no, no; it just cannot be."

About her death: "We are all saddened by Kathleen's death. . . . What a loss, and yet what a wonderful moment for the celebration of a life that has meant so much to so many. . . . Sorrow is not forever; love is. . . . Death must be right because it happens to all of us. . . . I am grateful for physical death when one's body cannot go on. . . . Hers is the victory, release from pain and suffering."

About Kathleen as a person: "I will always remember her as a kind, considerate, capable, special person. . . . She is a joy image in my memory bank. . . . She is well loved by the members of her church . . . always admired for her dedication and insight."

About her husband's feelings: "When I think about what I've lost, my pain is unbearable. When I think about what I have had, my joy is unutterable."

Dear friends, parallel testimonies could be said of the one we honor today. Let us all rejoice in a life so well lived, and be thankful for the privilege of sharing it. When someone so near and dear dies we habitually remark, "But think of what we have lost!"

Let us all think of what we have left, not what we have lost. The word *lost* is an emotional bomb that weakens resolve; it takes the wind out of our sails and fills our hearts with gloom.

Dr. Daniel Poling said on the occasion of his wife's death, "My dear wife is not lost. She is gone and I know where I can find her."

Ralph Waldo Emerson was once confronted by a wide-eyed lady who hurried down the aisle, seized him by the arm, and exclaimed, "Dr. Emerson, don't you know the world is coming to an end this year on October fourteenth?" Dr. Emerson calmly replied, "Oh, well, let it go. We can get along without it."

That's the way we Christians believe about the world and our body. We are in no hurry to leave it. This is a wonderful world. There is much to be done here for our Father. This is the best body we can live in here. But when we are called to leave it, it is not the end. Paul said, "For to me . . . to die is gain" (Philippians 1:21).

There is never an occasion in life in which everything is lost. There is always something and someone left.

Quiet your mind and heart right now and review what you have left:

You have breath and health
You have a home and friends
You have children and grandchildren
You have neighbors
You have a grand legacy
You have an occupation
You have faith and promise

See, already the clouds of grief are dispelling!

"I do not count the suffering of this world which is but for a moment, worth comparing to the glory that shall be . . ." (*see* Romans 8:18).

Pastoral Prayer

Heavenly Father, we thank You for the assurance that the one we loved is now with You. We thank You for the merciful release that has terminated her pain and fear.

Devastated by the loss, we pray for the comfort of thoughtful friends, precious memories, sustaining faith, and the perspective of eternal life. Into Thy hands we commend the keeping of both living and dead. May Thy peace attend us, now and forevermore, through Jesus Christ our Lord. Amen.

Postlude

"Goin' Home"
"Now Thank We All Our God"
"Now the Day Is Over"

13

FOR A YOUNG-PARENT CANCER VICTIM

Prelude

"O Holy Spirit, Comforter"
"Consolation," by Mendelssohn

Opening Sentences

Upon the door of our hearts, the Spirit of God knocks, in memories that make us glad, in gratitude that makes us humble, in compassion that opens the gates of generosity, in visions of the future that challenge our finest. Open the doors of the temple and let the Holy Comforter come in.

Invocation

High and eternal God, who has reached through the stable door into our experience, we know You in the Person and character of Jesus of Nazareth, who bore the image of Your Being. May this knowledge quiet our fretful hearts, deepen our trust, and give meaning to this death and our life, in Jesus' power. Amen.

Hymn (optional)

"The Lord's Prayer"

Old Testament Scripture Readings

General Selections:
Psalm 23
Psalms 46:1–5

Specifically Relevant Selections:

Better is a little with righteousness than great reve-
nues without right. A man's heart deviseth his way:
but the Lord directeth his steps. . . . How much better
is it to get wisdom than gold! and to get understanding rather to be chosen than silver! The highway of
the upright is to depart from evil: he that keepeth his
way preserveth his soul.

Proverbs 16:8, 9, 16, 17

The just man walketh in his integrity: his children
are blessed after him.

Proverbs 20:7

A good name is rather to be chosen than great
riches, and loving favour rather than silver and gold.

Proverbs 22:1

New Testament Scripture Readings

General Selections:
Romans 8:35, 37, 39
1 Corinthians 15:42–44
2 Corinthians 4:16–18; 5:1

Specifically Relevant Selections:

. . . And I therein do rejoice, yea, and will rejoice.
For I know that this shall turn to my salvation
through your prayer, and the supply of the Spirit of
Jesus Christ. According to my earnest expectation
and my hope, that in nothing I shall be ashamed, but
that with all boldness, as always, so now also Christ
shall be magnified in my body, whether it be by life,
or by death. For me to live is Christ, and to die is
gain.

Philippians 1:18–21

And the peace of God, which passeth all understanding, shall keep your hearts and minds through

Christ Jesus. . . . But my God shall supply all your
need according to his riches in glory by Christ Jesus.
Now unto God and our Father be glory for ever and
ever. Amen.

Philippians 4:7, 19, 20

Pastoral Prayer

Dear Lord, our minds cry out "why?" but our hearts say
"trust." In our humanness we cannot penetrate the cloud that
has fallen over us. Keep the candle of faith burning in our
hearts, our Father, so that we may follow the light, find meaning to existence, and experience the sun shining again.

We are thankful for the life and spirit of this young father.
How wise, controlled, and faithful he was. We marvel at the
fortitude, uncomplaining spirit, and patient endurance with
which he faced pain. We have been inspired by his faith. In
this he has made a profound witness that shall always be remembered. Now that his strife is over and release has come, we
commend him to you, O God, who art everlasting, loving, and
merciful. We pray for his wife and children a path strewn with
goodness, kindness, true friendships, and solace. Though cut
short by the father's death, may his fondest dreams for his family come to fruition, through Thy love in Jesus Christ. Amen.

Hymn (optional)

"It Is Well With My Soul"

Meditation

HE IS RISEN

Long, long years ago, the prophet Isaiah said to the priests,
" 'Comfort my people,' says our God. 'Comfort them! Encour-
age the people of Jerusalem. Tell them they have suffered long
enough and [they] . . . are now forgiven' " (Isaiah 40:1, 2 TEV).

At the start there is comfort in weeping. As clergymen we

are supposed to be grief experts and not to lose emotional control when dealing with situations like this. Some have conveyed that men of faith and good Christians should never weep, especially at death.

But I will have to admit that when the tragic news of _____'s death came to me, I was moved to tears, numbness and disbelief. Who can help it at a time like this? Did not Jesus Christ weep at the news that His friend Lazarus had died? And in the Garden of Gethsemane when He begged, ". . . If it be possible, let this cup pass from me: nevertheless not as I will, but as thou wilt"? (Matthew 26:39). And on the cross, when He cried out bitterly, ". . . My God, my God, why hast thou forsaken me?" (Matthew 27:46).

Something in weeping is important to give vent to our sorrow, to drain off the emotion in order that clarity, objectivity, strength, and healing comfort might result. God gave us the ability to cry for a reason—and this is it! Here is an atmosphere for you to weep in.

At one funeral I conducted, one of the daughters was attempting to be very brave, stoical, and hardened to the reality. After the service, she just burst into uncontrollable crying. Some tried to quiet her, but to no avail. It was precisely what she needed to do, to drain off the pent-up emotions of sorrow, anger, hostility, guilt, remorse, and all those other feelings that yearn for expression at a time like this. It is not weakness; it is a part of healing.

A woman lost her thirty-three-year-old son with cancer. He was married, father of two children, and dwindled to fifty-five pounds after months of indescribable suffering. The patient and the entire family revealed sterling qualities that helped them through the ordeal. I want to share a few quotes with you, for I am confident they can help sustain and comfort you.

The young parent himself said to his family on his death bed, "Don't cry for me; I don't need it. I'm going to miss you all very much, but what is ahead will be so good. Believe me."

His dad said, shortly afterward, "I don't know how people without God can meet death. Without Him, everything meaningful comes to its end."

The dad said that an eight-year-old nephew helped him as much as anyone with the following letter:

Dear Aunt Jo and Uncle J.C.,

I hope that you don't feel so bad about Junior. He is feeling better in heaven. He feels better up in heaven, because Junior is not suffering. I have been praying for Junior. My class has been praying for Junior also. If you can understand this, Junior is not really dead. Junior is just going into his last phase of his life. I know that he died at a young age. He was the same age as Jesus when Jesus died. Whatever God put Junior on this earth to do, Junior has already accomplished it. I hope this will make you feel better.

Love, Jason

There is quite a theologian and philosopher. It is a childish faith, but it is a Christian perspective. Such a view of death does help.

J.C.'s six-year-old grandson, whose neighbor died, said to his granddad after returning from the cemetery, "They talk like he is still there. He isn't, is he?"

Of course not! To a Christian, the cemetery is the emptiest place in the world. There is just nobody there. As the angel assured the bewildered disciples at the tomb on that first Easter, "He is not here. He is risen!" So dear friends, your loved one, the soul and spirit of your child, the real person that you have known and loved, is not here. He is risen!

When I was a youth I attended summer conference. Each day was closed with a friendship circle out under the stars. After a brief meditation and prayer we sang these words to the tune of "Taps":

Day is done, gone the sun
From the lake, from the hills, from the sky,
All is well, safely rest;
God is nigh.

Benediction

> Peace I leave with you, my peace I give unto you:
> not as the world giveth, give I unto you. Let not your
> heart be troubled, neither let it be afraid.
>
> John 14:27

Postlude

"Guide Me, O Thou Great Jehovah"

14

FOR A VEHICLE ACCIDENT VICTIM

Prelude

"Holy Spirit, Truth Divine"
"Spirit of God, Descend Upon My Heart"
"O Sacred Head, Now Wounded"

Opening Sentences

"Cast thy burden on the Lord, and he shall sustain thee . . ."
(Psalms 55:22). "He healeth the broken in heart, and bindeth
up their wounds" (Psalms 147:3). "Blessed are they that
mourn: for they shall be comforted" (Matthew 5:4).

Invocation

With broken hearts and forlorn spirits, we come before You,
O God, to be healed, comforted, and sustained. Dear Father,
by Your grace, grant us Your forgiveness, mercy, and comfort.
Enfold us within Your fellowship of love and in the household
of faith. Enlighten us in our seeking. Deepen us in our trusting.
Unravel our mixed-up, confused feelings so that we may face
what we must in a triumphant way, through Jesus Christ, the
Lord, Amen.

Hymn (optional)

"Because He Lives"
"I Know My Redeemer Lives"

Old Testament Scripture Readings

General Selections:
Psalms 55:22
Psalms 62:1, 2
Isaiah 40:1, 28–31

Specifically Relevant Selections:

> And the king was much moved, and went up to the chamber over the gate, and wept: and as he went, thus he said, O my son Absalom, my son, my son Absalom! would God I had died for thee, O Absalom, my son, my son!
>
> 2 Samuel 18:33

> The Lord is my light and my salvation; whom shall I fear? the Lord is the strength of my life; of whom shall I be afraid? . . . Wait on the Lord: be of good courage, and he shall strengthen thine heart: wait, I say, on the Lord.
>
> Psalm 27:1, 14

New Testament Scripture Readings

General Selection:
Romans 8:35–39

Specifically Relevant Selections:

> And we know that all things work together for good to them that love God, to them who are the called according to his purpose.
>
> Romans 8:28

> Beloved, I wish above all things that thou mayest prosper and be in health, even as thy soul prospereth

... Beloved, follow not that which is evil, but that which is good. He that doeth good is of God: but he that doeth evil hath not seen God.

3 John 1:2, 11

Pastoral Prayer

God, You have so mysteriously made us so that living in this temporal house we still may think Thy thoughts. We are but children of a day—our sun has its rising and its setting; yet deep within us we know the instinct of immortality and reach for eternity.

We thank You, dear God, for the gift of memory and for the ties that bind our hearts in love. We remember just now the one we have long loved and admired, who is now gone from our sight. His name is precious in our memory. His life was dear to our hearts. We feel a profound loss. Dear Lord, join to our company today his invisible presence, help us to believe in your infinite world where he is still alive, so that barren places may rejoice and the desert of our hearts may blossom again.

We thank You for the life of Jesus, giving visible expression to what we yearn for and to the quality of Your being. Merciful Father, forgive our contradictions, our neglect, our selfishness. Forgive what we have done that we should not have done and the things we have left undone that we should have done. Lord, help us inculcate Jesus into our hearts that we may share His abundant life, His resurrection, and His peace, which the world cannot take away. So may it be. Amen.

Hymn (optional)

"There Is No Sorrow, Lord, Too Light," verses 1–3

Meditation

BEAUTY WRAPPED AROUND TROUBLE

Paul the Apostle admonished us to comfort one another with the comfort wherewith we have been comforted.

In our losses, how have we been comforted? If we can remember what it was and who it was, perhaps we can convey that healing comfort to you, dear friends.

One source of comfort is memory. Mr. and Mrs. [parents' name], you have done a wonderful job in rearing your family. _____ was a good boy and it was to your credit; we all attest to that. We give you an A plus for your efforts in developing the qualities of character that endeared him to so many and made him so outstanding. [Enlarge here about personal qualities.]

Perhaps you second-guess the wisdom of giving him a vehicle and teaching him to drive. Like all parents you had ambivalent feelings. You weighed the matter. Driving a vehicle is a part of one's maturing, and most everything we do carries elements of risk.

Why this happened we cannot say anymore than we can answer why a tornado devastates a city or lightning kills a horse or an airplane is pulled from the sky by gravity. Rest assured that you did nothing to deserve this tragedy. Do not blame yourself. It will only destroy your peace of soul. It was because you loved him and wanted him to have some measure of joy and fun with his friends, and to become a useful, responsible, and independent citizen. After all, we parents cannot tie our children to the rocking chair. You did what parents are supposed to do. Look at the stars, not at the darkness. Remember the years of joy you had with him. Keep your memory green.

Also you may find comfort from your family and friends. I say, *may,* because not all are sources of comfort at such a time.

Recently a bereaved mother, through the Dear Abby column, gave us good advice in being comforters:

Dear Abby: My fourteen year old son was killed in a tragic accident seven months ago, and I am just now beginning to come out of shock. Throughout the ordeal, friends, family, and acquaintances tried to comfort me. Some succeeded, while others failed miserably.

The following comments are words that did not help at all. I realize that everyone was trying to be kind, but there are certain words bereaved parents do not want to hear:

1. "I know just how you feel. I lost my mother, father, husband, brother, etc. . . ." Unless you have suffered the loss of a child, there is no way you can know how another feels.

2. "It was God's will. . . ." If it was "God's will" to take my son at fourteen and end his young life, then I want no part of a God who could be so cruel.

3. "God needed him more than you did." How inadequate that made me feel. If I had needed him more, would he still be alive?

4. "These things happen for a reason." What reason? There is no reason good enough to explain to me why I had to suffer the loss of my child.

5. "You can have another child," or, "At least you have your other children." This is really cold and cruel. Children are individuals and no child can replace the child who died.

Now for some words that comforted me: a simple and heartfelt, "I'm so sorry." Many people hugged me, held my hand or cried with me. No words were spoken, but they were there for me when I needed them.

Linda Lancaster

Finally, there is comfort in the Holy Spirit of God.

Now that death has come to your son, there is no turning back. You cannot change the outcome. You can do one of two things: You can let this terrible thing destroy you with resentment, hostility, and anger—you can shake your fist at God and damn Him; or you can accept the heartache with trusting faith in God, faith in the resurrection to a continuing existence for development of soul, faith that this is not the end and someday you shall be reunited. What we see now is like a dim image in a mirror; then we shall see face-to-face. What we know now is only partial; then it shall be complete (*see* 1 Corinthians 13:12).

Learn from the lowly oyster. What does an oyster do the

moment a grain of sand invades its shell? Does it cry out,
"Why, with all the other billion of oysters up and down the
seashore, did this thing happen to me?" No, the oyster does not
openly complain. It sets itself to the task of enveloping the
grain of sand with a milky plastic substance that by and by is
made into a beautiful pearl. Peter Marshall once said "A pearl
is a thing of wonderful beauty wrapped around trouble."

The invasion of this painful experience, if surrounded by
faith, hope, and love, can transform your life and beautify your
character forever.

Benediction

May Almighty God, the Father, the Son, and the Holy Spirit
bless you and keep you, now and forever. Amen.

Postlude

"O Love That Wilt Not Let Me Go"
"Lead, Kindly Light"
"Abide With Me"

15

FOR A YOUNG MILITARY CASUALTY

Prelude

"Christ for the World We Sing"
"America the Beautiful"
"My Country, 'Tis of Thee"
"God Bless America"

Opening Sentences

God is our refuge and strength, a very present help
in trouble. Therefore will not we fear, though the

earth be removed, and though the mountains be carried into the midst of the sea; Though the waters thereof roar and be troubled, though the mountains shake with the swelling thereof. There is a river, the streams whereof shall make glad the city of God, the holy place of the tabernacles of the most High. God is in the midst of her; she shall not be moved: God shall help her, and that right early.

Psalms 46:1–5

Invocation

O God of all worlds, seen and unseen, transient and eternal; we quiet our minds that we may be still and know Thy presence. Divine Comforter, come close to each of us; beyond the power of any human prayer, meet Thou our inner needs. Bring life to our sagging spirits and let there be a resurrection of love and spirit and faith as we commend our loved one to Thy care, through Jesus Christ our Lord. Amen.

Reading of Military Citation

Hymn (optional)

"God of Our Fathers"

Old Testament Scripture Readings

General Selections:
    Psalms 27:1, 3–6, 13, 14
    Psalms 90:1–6, 10, 12–17

Specifically Relevant Selections:

Strengthen ye the weak hands, and confirm the feeble knees. Say to them that are of a fearful heart, Be strong, fear not: behold, your God will come with vengeance, even God with a recompence; he will come and save you. Then the eyes of the blind shall be opened, and the ears of the deaf shall be unstopped. Then shall the lame man leap as an hart, and the tongue of the dumb sing: for in the wilderness shall waters break out, and streams in the desert. And the parched ground shall become a pool, and the thirsty land springs of water: in the habitation of dragons, where each lay, shall be grass with reeds and rushes. And an highway shall be there, and a way, and it shall be called The way of holiness; the unclean shall not pass over it. . . . No lion shall be there, nor any ravenous beast shall go up thereon, it shall not be found there; but the redeemed shall walk there: And the ransomed of the Lord shall return, and come to Zion with songs and everlasting joy upon their heads: they shall obtain joy and gladness, and sorrow and sighing shall flee away.

Isaiah 35:3–10

Arise, shine; for thy light is come, and the glory of the Lord is risen upon thee. . . . The sun shall be no more thy light by day; neither for brightness shall the moon give light unto thee: but the Lord shall be unto thee an everlasting light, and thy God thy glory. Thy sun shall no more go down; neither shall thy moon withdraw itself: for the Lord shall be thine everlasting light, and the days of thy mourning shall be ended.

Isaiah 60:1, 19, 20

New Testament Scripture Readings

General Selections:
   John 11:25, 26
   Hebrews 12:1, 2

Specifically Relevant Selections:

For God sent not his Son into the world to condemn the world; but that the world through him might be saved.

John 3:17

For we know that the whole creation groaneth and travaileth in pain together until now. And not only they, but ourselves also, which have the firstfruits of the Spirit, even we ourselves groan within ourselves, waiting for the adoption, to wit, the redemption of our body. For we are saved by hope. . . .

Romans 8:22–24

. . . but hope that is seen is not hope: for what a man seeth, why doth he yet hope for?

Romans 8:24

Finally, my brethren, be strong in the Lord, and in the power of his might. Put on the whole armour of God, that ye may be able to stand against the wiles of the devil. For we wrestle not against flesh and blood, but against principalities, against powers, against the rulers of the darkness of this world, against spiritual wickedness in high places. Wherefore take unto you the whole armour of God, that ye may be able to withstand in the evil day, and having done all, to stand. Stand therefore, having your loins girth about with truth, and having on the breastplate of righteousness; And your feet shod with the preparation of the gospel of peace; Above all, taking the shield of faith, wherewith ye shall be able to quench all the fiery darts of the wicked. And take the helmet of salvation, and the sword of the Spirit, which is the word of God: Praying always with all prayer and supplication in the Spirit, and watching thereunto with all perseverance and supplication for all saints.

Ephesians 6:10–18

Pastoral Prayer

Merciful Father, who lovest every person as though there were but one to love, minister to these dear friends in their distress. Temper their sorrow with gratitude. Turn their thoughts from that which is lost to that which they can never lose, to the radiant charm of youth and the sanctifying memories of childhood. May thoughts of whatever was honorable and just, lovely and gracious, become a garment of praise to cover the spirit of heaviness. Beyond these consolations, add a clearer discernment of the meaning of life, not in its duration, but in its inspiration, not in the number of years but in the remembrance of deeds well done.

Merciful Father, forgive our sins of omission and commission. Deal with us tenderly. Help us to forgive one another. We cast ourselves upon thy mercy.

Set before us the appealing figure of the young Jesus, with His work, it seemed, unfinished and His life prematurely lost, dying with forgiveness on His lips and complete trust in His heart. May we hear His comforting message, "Peace I leave with you, my peace I give unto you . . ." (John 14:27). ". . . I have finished the work which thou gavest me to do" (John 17:4). So may it be. Amen.

Hymn (optional)

"We Would Be Building"

Meditation

I'LL LIVE FOR HIM

We are here to honor _____, who sacrificed his life for you and for me. He served honorably in the military of our country. Regardless of how you may feel about the military and our nation's involvements in conflict, it has been men like this one who have preserved our nation's freedom and peace and protected us from tyrannical forces. We mourn his death at such an untimely age and share the profound loss with you and his family.

We are proud of his valor and courage and are humbly grateful for his devotion to freedom. And now he truly has freedom.

Freedom
>   —from being driven,
>   —from fear,
>   —from seeking acceptance,
>   —from weariness,
>   —from a feeling that the task is impossible,
>   —from a feeling that communication is impossible,
>   —from wanting to change everything, immediately,
>   —from always wanting,
>   —from always wanting—freedom.[1]

Since his life was snuffed out at a tender age, you and I must live for him. We must live out his commitments, his spirit, his dreams.

An American Baptist named Dr. Edwin Dahlberg spoke frequently at church conventions. What an inspiration he was. At one of them he told of a personal influence that illustrates this point.

His Scandinavian parents came to the new world, settling in Minnesota. A brother two years his senior died as an infant at one year of age. He was laid to rest in the little cemetery back of the church, a familiar custom in past years. When his mother learned that she would again give birth to a child, she announced that she wished to call it, if a boy, by the name of her dead infant son, Edwin Dahlberg. And so she did. When this great preacher was born, he was given the name of his brother who preceded him. Dr. Dahlberg told the convention audience how all of his life he had gone back to that cemetery frequently to see his name on his brother's tombstone. He said it gave him a rather strange, yet wonderful feeling. He always felt that he had to live for his brother as well as for himself.

This is the way I want all of us to feel. This lad would not wish for you to spend the balance of your life in bitterness, cynically shaking your fist in God's face. I am certain he would say, "Live for me! Do the things I loved to do! Live, love, and laugh together." When you laugh, laugh a bit for _____. When you are having fun, remember to have a portion for him, too. If you love to play ball, swim, and dance, reserve a place for him. If you are doing things constructive, involved in achieving brotherhood, working for peace, and building a safe tomorrow, then you are living out his life already.

It is easy at a time like this to ask, "Why did he have to die so young?" We may be tempted to become bitter and hostile, saying, "Don't tell me there is a God of love and mercy, now that this has come to pass."

Remember, dear friends, that God's own Son, Jesus Christ, died at thirty-three as a result of unjust, inhuman, cruel behavior of misguided people—just like your son. Yet Christians for two thousand years have built upon this act of inhumanity, living out Jesus' life by carrying the gospel of love and peace, forgiveness and goodwill to the ends of the earth. Peter and James and John and countless disciples began to live a bit better and harder for their elder brother. So must we. May _____'s death point you to something greater, vaster, and lovelier.

One family's high-school son was killed just prior to his graduation. After the bitterness and grief subsided, they transformed that cruel catastrophe into a continuing blessing. In his name they gave money for a church camp building where boys and girls, men and women, in years to come might go to conference to learn, have fun, and become more like Jesus. Is that boy dead? No, he lives through the happiness, laughter, and lives of each successive person who attends that camp. You can keep your son living, too—through your deeds, commitments, and dedication.

There is an old gospel hymn we have sung, the text of which I trust will linger with you:

> I'll live for Him who died for me
> How happy then my life shall be!
> I'll live for Him who died for me,
> My Saviour and my God![2]

Benediction

God will give you light for your way, strength for your burdens; peace for your worries, forgiveness for your sins, love for your healing, hope for your future. So let us go forth to live for Him. Amen.

Postlude

"Lead On, O King Eternal"
"Largo," by Handel
"Now the Day Is Over"

16

FOR A GOOD PERSON WITH NO FORMAL RELIGIOUS COMMITMENT

Prelude

"Immortal, Invisible, God Only Wise"

Opening Sentences

Like the sun that is far away and yet close at hand to warm us, so God's Spirit is ever present and around us. Let not the clouds of depression or doubt, sorrow or guilt, keep the waves of God's Spirit from us. We open now the windows of our souls to God's presence.[1]

Invocation

Maker of all that we see and all that we do not see; greater than any and all parts of creation, yet no part is apart from You; produced neither by human will nor intellect, yet the producer of all human ability and compassion: You are the clue to our existence; You are the meaning in all experience; You are the center of the universe; You are the eternal One whom alone we can now trust, through Jesus Christ. Amen.

Old Testament Scripture Readings

General Selections:
  Ecclesiastes 3:1–8, 10
  Isaiah 40:28–31

Specifically Relevant Selections:

> A good name is better than precious ointment; and the day of death than the day of one's birth. It is better to go to the house of mourning, than to go to the house of feasting: for that is the end of all men; and the living will lay it to his heart.
>
> Ecclesiastes 7:1, 2

> Children are fortunate if they have a father who is honest and does what is right.
>
> Proverbs 20:7 TEV

> Do what is right and fair; that pleases the Lord more than bringing him sacrifices.
>
> Proverbs 21:3 TEV

> If you have to choose between a good reputation and great wealth, choose a good reputation.
>
> Proverbs 22:1 TEV

New Testament Scripture Readings

General Selections:
  Revelation 14:13
  1 John 4:16–21

Specifically Relevant Selection:

> "But when the Son of Man comes in his splendour with all his angels with him, then he will take his seat on his glorious throne. All the nations will be assembled before him and he will separate men from each other like a shepherd separating sheep from goats. He will place the sheep on his right hand and the goats on his left.

"Then the king will say to those on his right: 'Come, you who have won my Father's blessing! Take your inheritance—the kingdom reserved for you since the foundation of the world! For I was hungry and you gave me food. I was thirsty and you gave me a drink. I was a stranger and you made me welcome. I was naked and you clothed me. I was ill and you came and looked after me. I was in prison and you came to see me there.'

"Then the true men will answer him, 'Lord, when did we see you hungry and give you food? When did we see you thirsty and give you something to drink? When did we see you a stranger and make you welcome, or see you naked and clothe you, or see you ill or in prison and go to see you?'

"And the king will reply, 'I assure you that whatever you did for the humblest of my brothers you did for me.'"

Matthew 25:31–40 PHILLIPS

Pastoral Prayer

God eternal, Your mercy is wider than the sea; Your love is broader than the measure of man's mind; Your heart is most wonderfully kind; we cast ourselves upon Your grace.

We have come to honor _____ who was rich in good works. For the spirit of his heart, which motivated him to unselfish service, and the influences upon his disposition that directed him, we are grateful. We hear our Master's admonition, "Well done, good and faithful servant."

Yet we are mindful, O Lord, that it is not by good works that we are saved, but by Your grace. For Your loving-kindness, unmerited love, faithful generosity to us, which none can ever merit, we are humbly grateful. We can but trust Your love, O God.

Continue Your mercy to our departed friend, to his sorrowing family, and to all of us whose lives were touched by his being. Help us, dear Lord, to so emulate the Christ, that we may pass the test of love and receive grace upon grace, through Jesus Christ. Amen.

Hymn (optional)

"I Know Not What the Future Hath"

Meditation

BY THEIR FRUITS

When Socrates, the Greek philosopher, was told that he must prepare for death, he answered, "Know ye not that I have been preparing for death all of my life?"

The important questions to ask today are:

> Not how did he die
> But, how did he live?
> Not how much did he gain,
> But how much did he give?[2]

As most of you know, our friend's religion was not formal or orthodox. He had not been formally baptized in water or been a member of an organized body of believers. He had never been a church attender or a student of the Bible. This I regret, because I believe in the church as an instrument for transmitting the faith and for service to God. I believe the symbols and sacraments are important to life and are enormously significant. The fellowship of the committed is for most of us a mutual support and a family of faith.

However, our friend was ever ready to help an unfortunate youth, to stoop down to cleanse a dirty wound, to comfort a distraught parent, to give his time and money for community improvement. He was a modern-day Good Samaritan who did not belong to the Levites in the temple, yet he attended the least of those in need. He was not of the orthodox fraternity, yet in many ways he did what many orthodox churchmen often would not do.

It is my conviction that Jesus Christ would commend him as he did the ancient Good Samaritan, for it was he who said, "By their fruits ye shall know them."

In no sense is it my intention to downplay the role of the organized church or the need for Christian worship, study, and fellowship. Yet, I acknowledge here was a man who put into daily practice the unselfish service Jesus talked so much about. He was consciously or unconsciously influenced by the ethics of Jesus Christ, who said, ". . . Love thy neighbour as thyself" (Matthew 22:39). "By this shall all men know that ye are my disciples, if ye have love one to another" (John 13:35).

Edgar Guest, one of America's own beloved, down-to-earth poets, said it this way, "I'd rather see a sermon than hear one any day."

World renowned Nobel Peace Prize winner, Mother Teresa, the sacrificing nun of Calcutta, once paraphrased Jesus' famous words. It is as if she were speaking of the one in whose memory we are gathered:

> When I was hungry, you gave me to eat.
> When I was thirsty, you gave me to drink.
> When I was homeless, you opened your doors.
> When I was naked, you gave me your coat.
> When I was weary, you helped me find rest.
> When I was anxious, you calmed all my fears.
> When I was little, you taught me to read.
> When I was lonely, you gave me your love.
> When I was in prison, you came to my cell.
> When I was on a sick bed, you cared for my needs.
> In a strange country, you made me at home.
> Seeking employment, you found me a job.
> Hurt in a battle, you bound up my wounds.
> Searching for kindness, you held out your hand.
> When I was a Negro, or Chinese, or white, and
> Mocked and insulted, you carried my cross.
> When I was aged, you bothered to smile.
> When I was restless, you listened and cared.
> You saw me covered with spittle and blood,
> You knew my features, though grimy with sweat.

When I was laughed at, you stood by my side.
When I was happy, you shared in my joy.[3]

Who do you think proves to be a neighbor?
Who do you think is an extension of God in the world?
Who do you think shows real love for God and man?

Benediction

May the words of our mouths and the meditations of our hearts, the deeds of our hands, and the influence of our lives, be acceptable in Your sight, O Lord, our strength and our Redeemer. Amen.

Postlude

"Love Divine, All Loves Excelling"

17

FOR MULTIPLE DEATHS

Prelude

"Master, No Offering"

Opening Sentences

The Lord is my light and my salvation; whom shall I fear? The Lord is the refuge of my life; of whom then should I go in dread?

Psalms 27:1 NEB

Send forth thy light and thy truth to be my guide and lead me to thy holy hill, to thy tabernacle, then I shall come to the altar of God. . . .

Psalms 43:3, 4 NEB

Then shall your light break forth like the dawn and soon you will grow healthy like a wound newly healed; your own righteousness shall be your vanguard and the glory of the Lord your rearguard.

Isaiah 58:8 NEB

Invocation

Blessed art Thou, our God and Father of our Lord Jesus Christ, who has sent us on a journey and quickened within us a living hope for the dead. Amid our unspeakable sorrow, we greatly rejoice in the promise of an ". . . inheritance incorruptible, and undefiled, and that fadeth not away . . ." (1 Peter 1:4) given at the end of the journey for those who love and obey Thee, through Jesus Christ, the Lord. Amen.

Hymn (optional)

"I Do Not Ask, O Lord, That Life May Be"
"Because He Lives"

Old Testament Scripture Readings

General Selections:
Deuteronomy 31:8
Psalm 23
Psalms 39:4, 5, 7, 8, 12
Psalms 56:3, 4
Psalms 90:1–17

New Testament Scripture Readings

General Selections:
Hebrews 4:16
Hebrews 12:1, 2
1 Corinthians 15:20, 22
John 5:24–29

Pastoral Prayer

Thanks to Thee, O God, for these whom we have long loved and now have lost for a while. Their lives were dear to us; their names are precious in our memories. We remember them today.

Spirit of the living God, walk among these friends here and see the priceless love and cherished loyalty in their hearts. As we meet, we are aware of the company of unseen witnesses and these who have joined the invisible presence. We believe that no harm has come to them, that the souls of the righteous are in Thy hands.

Sustain their families and friends with this assuring faith, through Jesus Christ, our Lord. Amen.

Meditation

THE PILGRIM VIEW OF LIFE

Words come with difficulty at a time like this. None of us is able to express how we really feel. This tragedy has claimed the lives of an entire family [or group]. Each person was unique and precious. Each person should be eulogized. Each one is dear and loved of God. Let us with deep appreciation recall the life, character, personality, and contributions of each as I read the names [names and brief sentences about each].

"Finally, brethren, whatsoever things are true, whatsoever things are honest, whatsoever things are just, whatsoever things are pure, whatsoever things are lovely, whatsoever things are of good report; if there be any virtue, and if there be any praise, think on these things" (Philippians 4:8).

In Hebrews 11:13, 14 (RSV) we read, "These all died in faith ... having acknowledged that they were strangers and exiles on the earth. For people who speak thus make it clear that they are seeking a homeland." This affirms the biblical view of life as a journey, as a pilgrimage.

We live in tents. *Tents?* Aren't they for vacationers or refugees or displaced persons or transients? We have brick homes. We are here to stay. But however much we try to disguise it, we live in tents. You do not have to read the Bible to know it. We are all transients; we are all pilgrims. We are all moving along, strangers and exiles on earth.

The earth is not our home. We are by the grace of God only passing through, as if it were a journey, making a few brief resting places along the way. The Bible never regards the world as life's final destination. We are, as Hebrews' author indicates, "exiles" in a strange land, resident aliens, wanderers, living in temporary lodging, with no settled place of abode, seeking our homeland. Life is a journey from eternity, through space and time, to eternity. There is an ultimate end to which God is leading. Each day completes a stage of the journey; each day brings us closer to our final destination. So today we look beyond the sorrow and frustration of this tragedy to focus our vision upon our homeland in the blessed Kingdom of God. The author of Hebrews could say of the patriarchs, "People who speak thus make it clear that they are seeking a homeland." Their bodies wander through the earth, but their souls are ever at home with God.

It is the same view Paul had when he said, "we are a colony of heaven" (*see* Philippians 3:20), ever penetrating the earth's wilderness with God's love, ever controlled by God's rule, ever keeping in touch with the homeland. Then one glorious day the colonists return home. What a day of rejoicing!

Perhaps the picture of a family vacation is even more consoling. Visualize a family leaving to go to a beautiful resort. Beautiful trees and flowers grow there. Exciting things to do, for every person, abound. Many families with youngsters are there. Some visit for the entire summer; some stay until the chill of autumn or the white snow of winter sets in. Other families remain there for only a few days. Endearing friendships develop. Every day contains excitement and pleasure, though there are chores to do as well.

Periodically some of the group leaves sooner than the others, taking the boat back home. Others shed tears at their going and regret the early parting. Families are always sorry that they have to leave such a beautiful area. However, the tears are soon dried and those left behind take up as before.

One day you awake to the realization that the end of your

sojourn is in sight. The vacation is over. However much you want to stay, you must return home. You are saddened by the approaching end. What before seemed a long way off now has drawn close. You crowd as much pleasure in each day as possible. You feel so reluctant to go. Thoughts of leaving friends and thoughts of the rough, chopping lake haunt you. You dread it.

But as the day approaches, you begin to think of the beautiful things of home—of all your friends and the rest of your family. It is sad to leave your friends in the beautiful vacation land, yet you must take the boat back to where you belong. What a great day of rejoicing!

A preacher said at a funeral, "We must live in two worlds."

Afterward he was challenged by a businessman, "We are living in only one world. We do not know of any other world than this one."

"If you did believe in another world, would it make any difference?" the preacher responded.

"Of course. If I believed that, I would change every major policy before night."

Yes, we are on a journey to another world—our homeland. What difference should that view make in your living?

Hymn (optional)

"Guide Me, O Thou Great Jehovah"
"Goin' Home"
"I Feel the Winds of God Today"

Benediction

Keep us by Thy power through faith for salvation, and to Christ Jesus our Lord be glory and dominion for ever and ever. Amen.

Postlude

"Largo," by Handel

FOR A YOUTH

Prelude

"Blessed Assurance"
"Fairest Lord Jesus"

Opening Sentences

> The light of God surrounds us;
> The love of God enfolds us;
> The power of God protects us;
> The presence of God is with us;
> Wherever we are, God is![1]

Invocation

God, before whose knowledge all human hearts lie bare and open, let Your Spirit enter into us, so that new awareness may comfort us, new affections may support us, new forgiveness may heal us, new purposes may involve us, and new assurances may quicken us in Your mercy and love, through Jesus Christ, our Lord. Amen.

Hymn (optional)

"How Great Thou Art"
"Beautiful Saviour"

Old Testament Scripture Readings

General Selections:
Psalm 23
Isaiah 43:2

Specifically Relevant Selection:

> For the mountains shall depart, and the hills be removed; but my kindness shall not depart from thee, neither shall the covenant of my peace be removed, saith the Lord that hath mercy on thee.
>
> Isaiah 54:10

New Testament Scripture Readings

General Selections:
Hebrews 12:1, 2
Romans 8:31–35, 37–39

Specifically Relevant Selections:

> There is therefore now no condemnation to them which are in Christ Jesus. . . .
>
> Romans 8:1

> And we know that all things work together for good to them that love God, to them who are the called according to his purpose.
>
> Romans 8:28

Pastoral Prayer

Merciful God, none of us is able to fathom Your vast designs or the workings of this universe of our living. We are bowed down with sorrow and despair.

Dear Holy Spirit, come to these hearts now to temper their sorrow with gratitude. Turn the thoughts of our bereaved friends from that which is lost to that which they can never lose, to the memories of radiant youth, to the joys of maturing years, to the laughter of good times, to the intimate consolations. May the memories ever linger as a garment of praise to lift the spirits of heaviness. Add to their minds, dear Father, a meaning to existence realized in life's inspiration more than its duration, in its quality of integrity and character more than its number of years. Set before these friends the approaching figure of Jesus, your Son, our Lord, who with His work seemingly unfinished and His life prematurely and tragically cut short, in a short time fulfilled a long time, and who with His death, saved the world.

Let us all hear his unperturbed message, ". . . I have finished the work which thou gavest me to do" (John 17:4). "Peace I leave with you, my peace I give unto you" (John 14:27). Amen.

Meditation

THERE'S SOMETHING SPECIAL

"Since the time of Adam parents have been having sons—all types, shapes and varieties. Some are tall and lank, others are short and stocky. Some are extremely handsome, others are plain."[2]

Many of these sons have brought honor to the most humble homes; others have brought honor to the most elegant and prestigious homes.

For every son who has brought honor, another has brought dishonor. Some walk the straight and narrow; others break every law in the books. Some reverence God; others curse Him. This son brought honor to his family and to God.

God had a Son, a very special Son. He called Him Jesus. A strange, wonderful combination of humanity and deity. He got kicked around a lot in his abbreviated thirty-three years on earth, all because He insisted on righteousness and fair dealing. This Son, like all sons, was most special to His Father and dearly loved by His mother.

All sons are special to a mother, to a father, to a family. They may not make *Who's Who* or the various halls of fame, or be broadly known, or even be successful by worldly standards. Yet there is a remarkable pride in one who is flesh of your flesh, bone of your bone, blood of your blood, spirit of your spirit, a "chip off the old block."

What is so special about this boy, _____? Take a long look at him today and you will know. He was very special to his

parents, his family, church and community; _____ was a good
student [enlarge here]. He discovered that *helping people* was
his most satisfying activity.

The parents said to me, "We did not realize _____ helped so
many people until he died." One elderly woman said, "I was
honored that he brought his friends to our house many times
because he wanted us to know them."

A man said, "My wife is an invalid, and your son helped her
by calling her every week."

A young woman who worked with him said, "We talked a
lot about careers, and as a result I have decided to study for the
ministry."

"We were surprised," said the parents, "by the many ex-
pressions of concern and care from strangers and friends whom
he befriended. We are honored by the many good things the
people have told us about our son. It makes us aware of how
death must hurt those who have few or no friends."

Then the father said these significant words which he meant
with all of his heart, "I am so proud to have been _____'s father!"

We have remembered this young man with gratitude. We
also have come to affirm our faith beyond death. Paul the
Apostle, writing to the Romans said, "For I reckon that the
sufferings of this present time are not worthy to be compared
with the glory which shall be revealed in us" (Romans 8:18).

> God sent His Son, They called Him Jesus,
> He came to love, heal and forgive;
> He lived and died to buy my pardon,
> An empty grave is there to prove my Savior lives.

> Because He lives I can face tomorrow
> Because He lives all fear is gone;
> Because I know He holds the future,
> And life is worth the living, just because He lives.

> And then one day I'll cross that river,
> I'll fight life's final war with pain;
> And then as death gives way to vict'ry,
> I'll see the lights of glory and I'll know He reigns.

Because He lives I can face tomorrow
Because He lives all fear is gone,
Because I know He holds the future,
And life is worth the living, just because He lives.[3]

Hymn (optional)

"I Feel the Winds of God"
"Goin' Home"

Benediction

God, forgive my sniffling and whining,
Help me back on my feet
So that I in turn may extend my hand
And help others rise
Above their problems.

Postlude

"Jesus, Savior Pilot Me"

19

FOR A HANDICAPPED CHILD

Prelude

"Lead, Kindly Light"
"O Holy Spirit, Comforter"

Opening Sentences

Let us with confidence draw near to the fountain of grace,
that we may receive mercy and find support for this time of

need. "Blessed be God, even the Father of our Lord Jesus Christ, the Father of mercies, and the God of all comfort" (2 Corinthians 1:3).

Invocation

Eternal God, intimate Father, whose mercies are known on both sides of death, with reverent and submissive hearts we bow before You. You are everlasting. In Your knowledge is the future. In Your love are the provisions for sustaining life. In You is our hope. Grant that we may be lifted out of darkness and distress into the light and peace of Your presence, through the perspective of Jesus Christ. Amen.

Hymn

"The Strife Is O'er"
"The Lord Is My Shepherd"

Old Testament Scripture Readings

General Selection:
Isaiah 40:28–31

Specifically Relevant Selections:

When thou passest through the waters, I will be with thee; and through the rivers, they shall not overflow thee: when thou walkest through the fire, thou shalt not be burned; neither shall the flame kindle upon thee. For I am the Lord thy God. . . .
Isaiah 43:2, 3

Comfort ye, comfort ye my people, saith your God. . . . Thou art my servant; I have chosen thee, and not cast thee away. Fear thou not; for I am with thee: be not dismayed; for I am thy God: I will strengthen thee; yea, I will help thee; yea, I will uphold thee with the right hand of my righteousness. . . . For I the Lord

thy God will hold thy right hand, saying unto thee,
Fear not; I will help thee.

Isaiah 40:1; 41:9, 10, 13

New Testament Scripture Readings

General Selections:
  Matthew 18:1–6
  2 Corinthians 4:17, 18
  2 Corinthians 5:1–9

Specifically Relevant Selection:

> Likewise the Spirit also helpeth our infirmities: for
> we know not what we should pray for as we ought:
> but the Spirit itself maketh intercession for us with
> groanings which cannot be uttered. And he that
> searcheth the hearts knoweth what is the mind of the
> Spirit, because he maketh intercession for the saints
> according to the will of God.

Romans 8:26, 27

Pastoral Prayer

O Holy Father, whose mercies are from everlasting to everlasting, to Thee alone can we flee for refuge in our affliction,
trusting in the assurance of Thy love. From the grief that burdens our spirits, from the sense of solitude and loss, from the
doubt and fainting of the soul in its trouble, we turn to Thee.
Strengthen our feeble faith, comfort our hearts, and by the gospel of thy beloved Son speak peace to our souls.

We thank Thee for the eternal home of joy and love, where
children play and sing. Lift the thoughts of these parents beyond this earthly scene to the eternal abode where children are
the greatest in the Kingdom.

O God—help us all to keep within us the spirit of little children, knowing that our Lord promised such His blessing. May
we strive to remove from our world those things that would in-
jure little children, and may we strive to grow in wisdom and

stature, in favor with Thee and all men, through Jesus Christ, our Lord. Amen.

Hymn

"God Will Take Care of You"
"Near to the Heart of God"

Meditation

HEAVEN'S SPECIAL CHILD

It was a day of great rejoicing when [child's name] graced the home of our dear friends [parents' names]. It soon became obvious that things were not as they should be, that the child was born handicapped, meaning he would need constant medical attention, and extra tender love and care.

During his short years, he has been in and out of the hospital, where the doctors, hospital personnel, and parents have fought valiantly for his life. Literally scores of people have prayed, loved, and cared for him since his birth. All of us have marveled that he has lived this long, beyond the doctors' expectations. It has required a special mother and father, who have put the child's needs first, doing everything for him that possibly could be done. No expense was spared in the fight for his life. I speak for the entire community when I say that you are two of the most special people that we have ever known. Most of us would have crumbled under the load you have carried.

Was _____'s life in vain? William Cowper's verse tells us that "God works in a mysterious way His wonders to perform." This child's mission on earth was a special one, and already many wonders have been experienced. He has taught us how to have a greater compassion and concern for others. We will all have bigger hearts for the sick and the unfortunate because of him. May you all take comfort in the reassuring words of the Master who said, ". . . Inasmuch as ye have done it unto one of the least of these . . . ye have done it unto me" (Matthew 25:40).

Also during these difficult days your families became "closer than close." A community was united in concern. There has been a blending of all denominations' prayers at the very throne of God.

By this child's endurance of pain, medical tests, all kinds of support systems, and limiting mechanisms, we have been inspired to greater patience and learned better how to meet adversities.

In no way was his life in vain. None of us will forget this little fellow, whose mission continues in God's new world, freed at last from earth's handicaps, to develop the full potential for which he was given life.

An unknown author writes of "Heaven's Very Special Child":

> A meeting was held quite far from Earth
> "It's time again for another birth,"
> Said the angels to the Lord above
> "This special child will need much love
> His progress may seem very slow
> Accomplishments he may not show
> And he'll require extra care
> From the folks he meets way down there
> He may not run or laugh or play
> His thoughts may seem quite far away
> In many ways he won't adapt
> And he'll be known as handicapped
> So let's be careful where he's sent
> We want his life to be content
> Please, Lord, find parents who
> Will do a special job for you
> They will not realize right away
> The leading role they're asked to play
> But with this child sent from above
> Comes stronger faith and richer love
> And soon they'll know the privilege given
> On caring for this gift from Heaven
> Their precious charge, so meek and mild
> Is Heaven's very special child."

Benediction

May the grace of courage, gaiety, and tranquility with all such blessedness as belongs to the children of the Father in heaven, be yours, to the praise of eternal God. Amen.

Postlude

"Goin' Home" (Largo)
"Guide Me, O Thou Great Jehovah"
"Peace I Leave With You"

20

FOR A PREMATURE BABY

Usually this is a graveside service or a family meeting in a small chapel.

Opening Sentence

John Watson has written, "No little child has ever come from God and stayed a brief while, returning again to the Father, without making glad the home, and leaving behind some trace of heaven."

Invocation

Divine Father, giver of life, the knowledge of this little life and the anticipation for its arrival have filled this couple's hearts with awe, marvel, and joy. It has been a touch of wonder. For reasons we do not understand, this little life has been returned, denying us the privilege and joy of its companionship. Comfort the parents, we pray, as we commend the infant's future to Thy love, in the Spirit of Jesus. Amen.

Scripture Reading

> And they brought young children to him, that he
> should touch them: and his disciples rebuked those
> that brought them. But when Jesus saw it, he was
> much displeased, and said unto them, Suffer the little
> children to come unto me, and forbid them not: for of
> such is the kingdom of God. Verily I say unto you,
> Whosoever shall not receive the kingdom of God as a
> little child, he shall not enter therein. And he took
> them up in his arms, put his hands upon them, and
> blessed them.
>
> Mark 10:13–16

Meditation

THE WONDER OF IT ALL

We are here to share the disappointment of our dear friends,
_____, whose hopes have vanished in the night, whose dreams
have eluded fulfillment, whose little life of their love has been
snatched while hopeful arms were cradled in anticipation.

None of us is wise enough to understand the reasons for this
happening; we are human enough to weep with you in sorrow
and to tell you we share your loss and care for you.

New York City's Museum of Natural History contains a fas-
cinating exhibit of the embryonic development of a baby from
conception to birth. It portrays in nine plastic frames the
month by month stages of the fetus, and finally the miracle of
birth. Scientists are not in agreement when the life becomes a
self-conscious soul. But the genetic transmission of life and
characteristics is a mysterious wonder giving evidence of a divine Creator's wisdom and will. We bow in awe before the
mystery of God and life.

Sometimes in the process something may go wrong, so that
the conceived life cannot reach fulfillment. We do not know,
nor will we ever know perhaps, what caused this life to be
snuffed out. When there is a critical imperfection or when the
mother's life is threatened or an unexpected or unknown mal-

ady or injury, a miscarriage may be God's natural and merciful way of terminating a life before consciousness develops. As Job reads ". . . The Lord gave, and the Lord hath taken away . . ." (Job 1:21).

It is comforting to believe this to be so. Though you have planned and prayed for this child of your love, felt its movements, prepared its place in your home, and your arms ache for its warmth, yet if it was doomed to limitation and suffering, how much better that these hopes be burst now, than after years of tears, heartbreak, and agony.

"For now we see through a glass, darkly . . . some day we shall understand even as we are now understood" (*see* 1 Corinthians 13:12).

A little girl was sent to the store with specific instructions from her mother to come directly home after her purchases. She was duly cautioned not to play or linger along the way. She was more than two hours coming home, much to the distress of her anxious mother. "Where have you been? Where have you been?" scolded the mother. "I'm sorry, Mother. I know I am late, but Jane broke her doll and I had to stop and help her fix it." Mother countered, "And how could you help her fix that broken doll?" In her precious, childlike manner, the girl responded, "I really couldn't, but I sat down with her and helped her cry."[1]

This is why we have come today—to cry with you, dear friends. As the late Catherine Marshall reminded us, "God is never so beautiful as through the veil of tears."

Baby Sleeps

The baby wept
The mother took it from the nurse's arms,
And hushed its fears, and soothed
    its vain alarms,
    and baby slept.

Again it weeps,
And God doth take it from the mother's arms,
From present griefs, and future unknown harms,
    And baby sleeps.[2]

Now we commit the body to this city of the dead, made precious by memories of others that lie beneath these markers, but it is our privilege to commend his spirit to God's garden of souls to grow in His love and care.

Benediction

Now may the peace of God which passes all human understanding abide with you, now and forever. Amen.

21

FOR AN UNEXPECTED DEATH OF A SPOUSE OR PARENT

Prelude

"Great Is Thy Faithfulness"
"In the Hour of Trial"

Opening Sentences

When thou passest through the waters, I will be with thee; and through the rivers, they shall not overflow thee: when thou walkest through the fire, thou shalt not be burned; neither shall the flame kindle upon thee. For I am the Lord thy God, the Holy One of Israel, thy Saviour. . . .

Isaiah 43:2, 3

Invocation

Eternal God, from whom we have come, to whom we are going, Thou art the unseen companion all the days of our earthly pilgrimage; we seek Thy help this day when the road has turned suddenly rough and clouds shut out the light. We are grateful for the assurance that "yea, though I walk through the valley of the shadow of death, . . . Thou art with me" (Psalms 23:4). With that assurance we can face tomorrow, in Thy holy name. Amen.

Hymn (optional)

"Because He Lives"
"Take My Hand, Precious Lord"

Old Testament Scripture Readings

General Selections:
Isaiah 40:10
Isaiah 54:10
Psalms 27:1

New Testament Scripture Readings

General Selections:
John 14:15–17, 27
2 Corinthians 1:3, 4
1 Corinthians 15:53–58

Pastoral Prayer

Dear Lord, who art nearer than hands and feet, we pray for these dear people, so stunned by this death. They need Thy help. Please sustain them. We do not ask that their grief be removed, but that Thou will bind up their broken hearts. Sanctify for them every precious memory. Grant a keener awareness of Thy presence alongside them now, so that death may not seem more real than life, nor their loss greater than the gain that has come to their loved one.

Into Thy tender care we commit their future. As a father comforts his children, so comfort these. Heavenly Father, as your own heart was pierced when Thy Son was put to death for our sakes, so may you feel the infirmities of us all and save us at last, through Jesus Christ, in whom is eternal life. Amen.

Hymn (optional)

"There Is a Balm in Gilead"
"The Lord's Prayer"

Meditation

THE MIRACLE OF SUSTAINING POWER

The Bible warns us how fleeting life can be. It is like grain that is here today and gone tomorrow or a vapor that is present and then fades. The years of life are ". . . soon cut off, and we fly away" (Psalms 90:10). "Boast not thyself of to morrow; for thou knowest not what a day may bring forth" (Proverbs 27:1).

We have known that, yet we had no inkling or premonition of the sudden way death would snatch away the life of _____.

We share this great loss with our dear friends. We recall with profound appreciation his life [enlarge here about personal facts and his contributions]. None can understand the deep emotions that our friends have experienced. The reality is hard for us to comprehend. The paralyzing grief we share.

However, even in the midst of suffering is the promise of holy comfort. In the throes of grief, there is a power from God to give you strength to go on living and to help you assimilate the loss.

Rabbi Harold Kushner, who has written so lucidly of the human predicament, says that on Father's Day, his daughter gave him a T-shirt to wear when jogging. On the back she had imprinted Isaiah 40:31 which reads, "They that wait upon the Lord shall renew their strength . . . they shall run, and not be weary; and they shall walk, and not faint."

He says, "After sharing so much sorrow, I still believe in the goodness of God and His world. I have seen people reach the limits of their own endurance, drain themselves dry of compassion, loyalty, and patience because life has asked so much from them. Then from a source somewhere beyond themselves, they gain a sudden infusion of new strength and new hope, so that they can continue to "run and not be weary, walk and not grow faint."[1]

People go through times when they are spiritually dead, lifeless, depressed—such as the time of sickness, death, and betrayal. Then they come to life again. God, who gives new life to the earth in springtime, sends the miracle of renewed life to His children as well.

We constantly see ordinary people do extraordinary things, like a couple who gave birth to a severely brain-damaged son. Against everybody's advice, they took the son home and raised him. Over the years they have shown more love and patience than one would imagine any family having. God renews strength so we can go on walking.

What does the familiar line from the Twenty-third Psalm say? "Yea, though I walk *through* the valley of the shadow of death . . ." (verse 4, *italics added*). God is most with us not when we linger among the shadows, but when we walk *through* them and come out on the other side.

A widow in her forties had never signed a check in her life. She had been totally dependent upon her husband who died suddenly. She had to take over his business. She was overwhelmed, desperate, angry, totally confused, and unprepared for what she was being asked to do. She would cry herself to sleep night after night, then awake in the morning, feeling drained and empty. But she persisted. People were patient with her while she learned. Today she is a respected figure and a more complete person than ever before.

Chapter thirty-two in Genesis describes how Jacob wrestled with a mysterious being and limped away from the encounter. But a few verses later he is described as being "whole" in a way he had never been before, not because he recovered from the ordeal, but because he distilled a special blessing from it.

We need the feeling that life is an adventure, a river leading somewhere. We need to see our days as containing the promise of something new, that the darkness of night always gives way to daylight, that when winter comes, spring cannot be far behind.

God gives us assurance, in his resurrection of Jesus from the dead, that there is the ultimate triumph of light over darkness, of hope over futility, of patience over despair, and of life over death. Praise be to God!

Benediction

Now may you be assured by the power of God, that after the scars come the stars, after the night comes a new day, after winter comes spring, after the cross comes the resurrection, after death comes eternal life, after the struggle comes peace.

So may it be to you as Christ's Spirit works within your heart. Amen.

Postlude

"Abide With Me"
"Peace, Peace, Wonderful Peace"

22

FOR A WORKER WITH SMALL CHILDREN

Prelude

"Immortal, Invisible, God Only Wise"

Opening Sentence

O come, open your heart to the love of God, nourish your mind with the truths of God, purify your imagination by the beauty of God, quicken your conscience by the holiness of God, surrender your will to the purpose of God—and you shall be comforted and strengthened and ennobled by the Giver Supreme.

Invocation

Infinite God, beyond the borders of our highest thoughts, beyond the edges of our sight, Your Being stretches; we keep open the end of our faith, believing where we cannot prove and walking where we cannot see, trusting goodness, love, and meaning in this experience as demonstrated by Jesus Christ, our Lord. Amen.

Hymn (optional)

"The King of Love My Shepherd Is"

Old Testament Scripture Readings

General Selection:
Psalm 23

Specifically Relevant Selection:

Hear, O Israel: The Lord our God is one Lord: And thou shalt love the Lord thy God with all thine heart, and with all thy soul, and with all thy might. And these words, which I command thee this day, shall be in thine heart: And thou shalt teach them diligently unto thy children, and shalt talk of them when thou sittest in thine house, and when thou walkest by the way, and when thou liest down, and when thou risest up. And thou shalt bind them for a sign upon thine hand, and they shall be as frontlets between thine eyes. And thou shalt write them upon the posts of thy house, and on thy gates.

Deuteronomy 6:4–9

New Testament Scripture Readings

General Selections:
John 14:1–3
John 11:25, 26

Specifically Relevant Selections:

Beloved, now are we the sons of God, and it doth not yet appear what we shall be: but we know that, when he shall appear, we shall be like him; for we shall see him as he is. And every man that hath this hope in him purifieth himself, even as he is pure.

1 John 3:2, 3

Beloved, think it not strange concerning the fiery trial which is to try you, as though some strange thing happened unto you: But rejoice, inasmuch as ye are partakers of Christ's sufferings; that, when his glory shall be revealed, ye may be glad also with exceeding joy. If ye be reproached for the name of Christ, happy are ye; for the spirit of glory and of God resteth upon you: on their part he is evil spoken of, but on your part he is glorified. But let none of you suffer as a murderer, or as a thief, or as an evildoer, or as a busybody in other men's matters. Yet if any man suffer as a Christian, let him not be ashamed; but let him glorify God on this behalf.

1 Peter 4:12–16

Pastoral Prayer

Dear Lord, we unite our spirits in expressing appreciation for the life of _____. With unconscious ways, her shadow has touched many lives with wholesome love and constructive guidance. We all have been blessed by her friendship.

Dear Lord, we recognize that we are but children of a larger order. Within us are amazing possibilities—abilities that have never been developed, seeds that have never been watered and so have never grown, latent spiritual powers slumbered to uselessness. O God, cause us to develop and grow into the persons you dream for us. We are but children or at best adolescents in our development. So grant us a new awareness and spiritual maturity as we face the trials and struggles of life.

Bless this family who feels this loss most profoundly. May it serve to enrich them in a deepened faith, a broadened sympathy, and far-reaching love, through Jesus Christ. Amen.

Meditation

THE NURSERY OF HEAVEN

We are here to honor the life of _____, who served as the director of the nursery and teacher in the day-care center. How she loved children! From her, children learned what love is, how to share with others, and received tender, loving care. Parents knew that the babies would have kind personal attention and toddlers and older ones could be assured of having a good time and would want to return.

It was truly the "nursery of heaven," for Jesus said, regarding children, "Of such is the Kingdom of heaven." We will all miss her very much, especially the children who loved her.

Your children will ask, "Where is _____? Where has she gone?" Perhaps we could explain that she has graduated beyond the nursery to a higher grade in God's eternal university.

Dr. Ralph Sockman once wrote, "The more I study the gospels, the more I think of our passage to the next life as through a schoolroom rather than a courtroom." We are accustomed to hear in dramatic fashion of death ushering us into a great court, before the Universal Judge, as condemned sinners who have only Jesus Christ to defend or ransom us.

I like to think of the future life as an extension of the courses we have taken here. A person will carry over into the world on the other side of death the qualities of Spirit developed here. Death will not arrest one's development; rather it is graduation time, the leaving of one level and the commencing of a higher one.

With this view, the world is a nursery of heaven, or at best, an elementary school in which the lessons of love, truth, and beauty are learned, in which God is known in the human life of Jesus. This is an antechamber to the vast university of eternity in which there are progressive degrees of faith, holiness, and character. As we strive to become "perfect as our heavenly Father is perfect" (*see* Matthew 5:48) we want to know more of God. "Now we see through a glass, darkly; . . . but then shall I know even as also I am known" (1 Corinthians 13:12).

If we have learned to like what Christ liked, if we have learned much of good in this life, if we are inclined toward God and Christlikeness, then it will be "heavenly." "God Himself will be with them." However, if we are uncomfortable with righteousness, are unfamiliar with God's ways, we shall be miserable. If we consciously have resisted Christ, we shall be separated from God. As the author of Acts records concerning Judas Iscariot, "He went to his own place" (*see* Acts 1:25). With twisted thoughts, perverted reasoning, and distorted values, he found his own level—the hell of being himself. He experienced the ashes of loneliness, the fires of remorse, the burning shame of guilt, the emptiness of separation. In contrast, Jesus said to His followers, ". . . I go to prepare a place for you" (John 14:2). You can be assured of existence beyond this life, for no one has exhausted his or her possibilities. Life goes on.

It is not wishful thinking. It is not illogical. All religions teach in some fashion of life going on. Christ stands above them all to say, with the assurance of resurrection, "Because I live, you, too, shall live." He said to the person next to him on the cross, "To day shalt thou be with me in paradise" (Luke 23:43). He did not say, "I hope" or, "There is a chance." He said it with certainty, "To day."

I can't prove it; however, experience verifies it. As little children, we all no doubt found a bird's nest, with perhaps an egg in it to be hatched. Within the egg was an embryo with amazing capabilities. It was shut in within a structure. Not until the shell was broken could the bird escape, take wings, and become what it was capable of becoming.

Just so, all that we know here on earth is embryonic, only partially developed, imperfectly expressed. We are immature, our faculties have greater capacities. By death, we break out of the shell that has limited us.

If this life is all there is, if we are allowed to develop friendships, love, and character, then suddenly it is all destroyed, this is an irrational universe, a meaningless existence.

Or carry the illustration to the baby. If in the prenatal days a baby could take voice, he might say, "I don't want to be born. I am warm, protected, and happy. In fact, I don't believe there is another world beyond this." But the fetus continues to develop, even within the limitations. One day he is born, escaping the confinement. His eyes are open. He is introduced to new worlds of sight, sound, color, and thoughts. He looks into the happiest faces ever known and grows into who can know what glory!

You see, the child might look at birth as we do death. Death is the entrance into another level, a graduation into another classroom, into the eternal university of God.

Kenneth Foreman pictures an arrival in heaven who was asked, "What would you like to be up here?" The soul answered with great enthusiasm, "I want to be a saint in Glory." The questioner asked, "What experience have you had?"

Our journey on this planet is as in the nursery of heaven. Our task is to learn that love, compassion, and joy that befits God. Our future depends upon it!

My Task

To love someone more dearly every day
To help a wandering child to find his way
To ponder o'er a noble thought and pray
And smile when evening falls
This is my task.

To follow truth as blind men long for light,
To do my best from dawn of day till night
To keep my heart fit for His holy sight
And answer when He calls
This is my task.

And then my Saviour by and by to meet
When faith has made this task on earth complete
And lay my homage at the Master's feet
Within the jasper walls
This crowns my task.[1]

Benediction

Now may God, who loves us and gives us eternal comfort
and good hope through grace, comfort your hearts and establish them in every good work, through Jesus Christ our Lord.
Amen.

Postlude

"The Funeral March," Chopin

23

FOR A MILITARY VETERAN

Prelude

"God of Our Fathers"

Opening Sentences

Let us worship God. Our help is in the name of the Lord,
who made heaven and earth, who is everlasting to everlasting.
The eternal God is your refuge and underneath are the everlasting arms.

Invocation

Living God, our Heavenly Father, Thou art the source of
our life, and Thou art the destiny of our pilgrimage. We have
come into Thy presence this day with hearts that are weary and
heavy laden. But in Thee we have refuge from the storms of
life. O Thou Good Shepherd, lead us now beside the still waters. Restore our souls. Deepen our flickering faith and renew
the love that never fails, in Jesus Christ, our Lord. Amen.

Old Testament Scripture Readings

General Selection:
  Psalms 90:1–6, 10, 12

Specifically Relevant Selection:

I will love thee, O Lord, my strength. The Lord is
my rock, and my fortress, and my deliverer; my God,
my strength, in whom I will trust; my buckler, and
the horn of my salvation, and my high tower. I will
call upon the Lord, who is worthy to be praised: so
shall I be saved from mine enemies. The sorrows of
death compassed me, and the floods of ungodly men
made me afraid. The sorrows of hell compassed me
about: the snares of death prevented me. In my distress I called upon the Lord, and cried unto my God:
he heard my voice out of his temple, and my cry came
before him, even into his ears.

Psalms 18:1–6

New Testament Scripture Readings

General Selection:
  Revelation 21:1–7

Specifically Relevant Selection:

Finally, my brethren, be strong in the Lord, and in
the power of his might. Put on the whole armour of
God, that ye may be able to stand against the wiles of
the devil. For we wrestle not against flesh and blood,
but against principalities, against powers, against the
rulers of the darkness of this world, against spiritual
wickedness in high places. Wherefore take unto you
the whole armour of God, that ye may be able to
withstand in the evil day, and having done all, to
stand. Stand therefore, having your loins girt about
with truth, and having on the breastplate of righ-

teousness; And your feet shod with the preparation of the gospel of peace; Above all, taking the shield of faith, wherewith ye shall be able to quench all the fiery darts of the wicked. And take the helmet of salvation, and the sword of the Spirit, which is the word of God. . . .

Ephesians 6:10–17

Pastoral Prayer

Gracious Father, we thank Thee for these words of assurance. We confess the mystery of life and death; the shock of death has invaded us, but in the depth of our sorrow we remember Jesus Christ, dying in the vigor of His manhood, yet living to be our comfort, our friend, and our assurance beyond death.

We thank Thee our Father for the life of _____, whom we loved and who has now gone closer to Thy presence. We appreciate all that was good, all that was kind, all that was worthy. For every good influence from his life, for his military leadership and dedication in preserving freedom, for the fatherly counsel to his fine children, for his disciplined principles, for the gift of his friendship, and his love for the church—we thank Thee, O God. Wherein he fell short, as we all do, be Thou merciful. Forgive us for deeds left undone and for sins done that should not have been done. O Lord, sustain, we pray, his wife with the remembrance that love can never die, with courage of faith, and with the comfort of devoted friends. Deepen the gratitude and humility of the children for the legacy that is theirs and give them a spirit of unselfishness.

Lead, kindly Light, until the shadows flee away, and the eternal day dawns, and we are reunited in Thee, through Jesus Christ. Amen.

Hymn (optional)

"O God, Our Help in Ages Past"
"God Bless America"

Meditation

PASSING OF THE TORCH

One of the meaningful national holidays is Veteran's Day, November eleventh. It began as Armistice Day, celebrating the conclusion of World War I, a sober reminder of the thousands upon thousands of American GIs who made the supreme sacrifice to preserve freedom.

In my early ministry I was constantly called upon to lead services on that date in the local school auditorium or at the civic center or at the cemetery. It was not so much a holiday as a holy day. It seemed many of the townspeople and students felt obliged to attend. It was a deliberate recall of the cost of our freedom. It began with the national anthem, played as the flag was raised; there was a firing squad and taps, then a minute of total silence, followed by a patriotic speech. It was a service of appreciation and remembrance for those who fought in the "war to end all wars" and those who subsequently fought in the "war that would save the world for democracy." Many thousands died, many more thousands were wounded and returned to live out their lives. O Lord, help us "lest we forget, lest we forget."

This service today is meant to recall one of those military veterans, _____, who, as a young man, sensed the urgent problem, heard his country call for volunteers, and was willing to go and to give himself. [Enlarge here if you wish, regarding his military service, awards, and other attainments in life.]

John McCrae wrote the immortal poem "Flanders Fields," in which he imagines one of the American doughboys buried in the Flanders Fields Cemetery in France, taking voice and saying:

> In Flanders fields the poppies blow
> Between the crosses, row on row,
>   That mark our place; and in the sky
>   The larks, still bravely singing, fly,
> Scarce heard amid the guns below.

We are the Dead. Short days ago
We lived, felt dawn, saw sunset glow,
    Loved and were loved, and now we lie
    In Flanders fields.

Take up our quarrel with the foe;
To you from falling hands we throw
    The torch; be yours to hold it high!
    If ye break faith with us who die
We shall not sleep, though poppies grow
    In Flanders fields.[1]

Hymn (optional)

"Sleep Thy Last Sleep"

Benediction

And the peace of God, which passeth all understanding, shall keep your hearts and minds through
Christ Jesus.

Philippians 4:7

Postlude

"It Is Well With My Soul"

24

FOR A WELL-KNOWN COMMUNITY LEADER

Prelude

"God of Our Fathers"
"Forward Through the Ages"

Opening Sentences

O come, let us worship and bow down: let us kneel before the Lord our maker. For he is our God; and we are the people of his pasture, and the sheep of his hand. . . .

Psalms 95:6, 7

Invocation

O hidden Source of life, the uncreated mind behind all creation, whose presence is hidden behind the clothes of nature, to whom the trees and flowers are ornaments to accent the beauty of Your Being, who is like a hand in the glove of the universe, we reach out to You in spirit and thought and faith, believing You feel our sorrows, hear our prayers, and provide for our needs, here and hereafter, as promised by Jesus Christ, lover of our souls. Amen.

Hymn (optional)

"Something Beautiful"

Old Testament Scripture Readings

General Selections:
Psalms 62:1, 2
Psalms 90:1, 2, 4–6, 12, 14, 16, 17

Specifically Relevant Selection:

And, behold, a certain lawyer stood up, and tempted him, saying, Master, what shall I do to inherit eternal life? He said unto him, What is written in the law? how readest thou? And he answering said, Thou shalt love the Lord thy God with all thy heart, and with all thy soul, and with all thy strength, and with all thy mind; and thy neighbour as thyself. And he said unto him, Thou hast answered right: this do, and thou shalt live. But he, willing to justify himself, said unto Jesus, And who is my neighbour? And Jesus answering said, A certain man went down from Jerusalem to Jericho, and fell among thieves, which stripped him of his raiment, and wounded him, and departed, leaving him half dead. And by chance there came down a certain priest that way: and when he saw him, he passed by on the other side. And likewise a Levite, when he was at the place, came and looked on him, and passed by on the other side. But a certain Samaritan, as he journeyed, came where he was: and when he saw him, he had compassion on him, And went to him, and bound up his wounds, pouring in oil and wine, and set him on his own beast, and brought him to an inn, and took care of him. And on the morrow when he departed, he took out two pence, and gave them to the host, and said unto him, Take care of him; and whatsoever thou spendest more, when I come again, I will repay thee. Which now of these three, thinkest thou, was neighbour unto him that fell among the thieves? And he said, He that shewed mercy on him. Then said Jesus unto him, Go, and do thou likewise.

Luke 10:25–37

Pastoral Prayer

Dear God, who has inspired and led men in all ages to lead others, we thank You for moulding _____ into a worthy public servant in this community. We acknowledge his many honorable qualities and our debt to him for the constructive leadership in this city. We are grateful that he was a man of deep religious convictions, who stood for the right, and was faithful in his efforts to build righteousness into the fabric of this city.

We all feel a profound loss, and we share the sorrow of his wife and family. Dear Lord, keep his influence ever expanding among us as we take up the mantle of service. We commend his keeping to Thee, O Lord, confident in the resurrection, through Jesus Christ. Amen.

Meditation

KEEPING MEMORY GREEN

In the thirteenth chapter of Exodus and the nineteenth verse is found this brief, seemingly insignificant statement, "And Moses took the bones of Joseph with him. . . ." It is filled with profound meaning, which has relevance for us today.

The children of Israel had lived under the whip and lash of the Egyptian slavemasters for a period of four hundred years. Then, from among the Hebrews, God raised up Moses to lead them from their bondage, organize them into a nation, and take them to the freedom of the Promised Land. After Moses attempted to negotiate their release with the pharaoh, aided by ten God-directed plagues, the time of their departure finally came. Moses commanded the slaves to pack quickly and secretly, and when the hour approached, to make haste to leave. The Bible indicates that within hours nearly a million Israelites moved out of Egypt: "And Moses took the bones of Joseph with him . . ."!

Why drag along the bones of a patriarch who had been dead for two centuries? Well, Joseph was the little Jewish boy who was sold by his jealous brothers in Palestine to Egyptian tradesmen who, in turn, took him to Memphis. With his ability and talent, Joseph, upon maturity, became a statesman, the prime minister no less of Egypt. In this favored position, led by his faith in almighty God, he brought his Jewish kinsmen to Egypt when a famine threatened their existence. Joseph excelled in faith, in moral practice, in wisdom. They must take his bones with them on the forty-year journey, so they would not forget his righteousness, his leadership, his salvation, and his faith in and dependence upon the one true God. "Moses took the bones of Joseph with him. . . ." By this recall they would know they were a keeper of destiny.

Today, we figuratively carry the bones of _____ with us as a constant reminder of the kind of man and leader he was.

We take his bones with us to remind us of responsibility and courage. We take his bones with us to remind us of righteousness and fairness, to remind us of magnanimity and forgiveness, to remind us of compassion and unselfishness. We take his bones with us to remind us of integrity and brotherly kindness, to remind us of patience and self-control, to remind us of faith and loyalty to God.

We are profoundly indebted to this great man. He moved us on our way to the Promised Land and pointed us in the right direction. We take his bones with us "Lest we forget, lest we forget!"

Charles Dickens once wrote a story entitled "The Tale of a Chemist." The plot centers around a chemist who was terribly bothered about his past. A phantom offered to take away his memory, assuring him that it would save him from guilt and remorse and thus become a great blessing. So the chemist yielded to the shock treatment that completely obliterated the past. However, what was promised to be a great blessing was indeed a damaging curse. He no longer understood who he was. His life had no depth, because he had no sense of history. His life had no direction, because he was unaware of continuity. All of life was immediacy. His relationships had no meaning, because they had no dimensions. The story closes with the chemist praying, "O Lord, keep my memory green." Keep our recall alive. Give us a sense of history that we might have appreciation and know who we are and where we are going.

"O Lord, keep our memory green." Let us take the bones of Joseph with us.

Hymn (optional)

"Now Praise We Great and Famous Men"

Benediction

". . . Brethren, give diligence to make your calling and election sure . . . For so an entrance shall be ministered unto you abundantly into the everlasting kingdom of our Lord and Saviour Jesus Christ" (2 Peter 1:10, 11), in whose name we pray. Amen.

Postlude

"Now Thank We All Our God"

25

FOR A POLITICAL STATESMAN

Prelude

"All Creatures of Our God and King"
"Thine Is the Glory"

Opening Sentences

Enter into his gates with thanksgiving, and into his courts with praise: be thankful unto him, and bless his name. For the Lord is good; his mercy is everlasting; and his truth endureth to all generations.

Psalms 100:4, 5

Invocation

O God, Author of eternal light, lead us in this service that our lips may praise Thee, our lives may bless Thee, our meditations may glorify Thee, through Jesus Christ, our Lord. Amen.

Hymn (optional)

"God of Grace and God of Glory"

Old Testament Scripture Readings

General Selections:
Psalm 1
Joshua 1:1, 2, 5, 7, 9

Specifically Relevant Selection:

Now these are the commandments, the statutes, and the judgments, which the Lord your God commanded to teach you, that ye might do them in the land whither ye go to possess it: That thou mightest fear the Lord thy God, to keep all his statutes and his commandments, which I command thee, thou, and thy son, and thy son's son, all the days of thy life; and that thy days may be prolonged. Hear therefore, O Israel, and observe to do it; that it may be well with thee, and that ye may increase mightily, as the Lord God of thy fathers hath promised thee, in the land that floweth with milk and honey.

Hear, O Israel: The Lord our God is one Lord: And thou shalt love the Lord thy God with all thine heart, and with all thy soul, and with all thy might. And these words, which I command thee this day, shall be in thine heart: And thou shalt teach them diligently unto thy children, and shalt talk of them when thou sittest in thine house, and when thou walkest by the way, and when thou liest down, and when thou risest up. And thou shalt bind them for a sign upon thine hand, and they shall be as frontlets between thine eyes. And thou shalt write them upon the posts of thy house, and on thy gates.

Deuteronomy 6:1–9

New Testament Scripture Readings

General Selection:
Hebrews 11:1–5, 7

Specifically Relevant Selections:

But Jesus called them to him, and saith unto them, Ye know that they which are accounted to rule over the Gentiles exercise lordship over them; and their great ones exercise authority upon them. But so shall it not be among you: but whosoever will be great among you, shall be your minister: And whosoever of you will be the chiefest, shall be servant of all.

Mark 10:42–44

For the grace of God that bringeth salvation hath appeared to all men, Teaching us that, denying ungodliness and worldly lusts, we should live soberly, righteously, and godly, in this present world; Looking for that blessed hope, and the glorious appearing of the great God and our Saviour Jesus Christ; Who gave himself for us, that he might redeem us from all iniquity, and purify unto himself a peculiar people, zealous of good works.

Titus 2:11–14

For this cause I bow my knees unto the Father of our Lord Jesus Christ, Of whom the whole family in heaven and earth is named, That he would grant you, according to the riches of his glory, to be strengthened with might by his Spirit in the inner man; That Christ may dwell in your hearts by faith; that ye, being rooted and grounded in love, May be able to comprehend with all saints what is the breadth, and length, and depth, and height; And to know the love of Christ, which passeth knowledge, that ye might be filled with all the fulness of God.

Ephesians 3:14–19

Pastoral Prayer

Lord and God of all history, who has raised up prophets and kings, statesmen and leaders, to direct Your people according to Your will, we pause in gratitude for Thy servant _____. Through good times and bad, in prosperity and adversity, in peace and war, he has been vigilant in representing the people, devoted to supporting legislation for the common welfare, sensitive to the demands of righteousness and integrity.

We commend his keeping to Thee, the Everlasting One, trusting Your mercy, love, and righteousness. We do not know what the future holds, but we know You hold the future, so we are not afraid.

Bless his wife and family with comfort from pride in his life, with assurance of resurrection, with true and understanding friends, and with deep, abiding faith in Jesus Christ, our Lord. Amen.

Meditation

A MIGHTY OAK HAS FALLEN

On the occasion of the death of Texas senator Sam Rayburn, Senator Tom Corcoran of New Hampshire wrote a letter to his colleague Lyndon Baines Johnson, then presiding over the Senate. He quoted Oliver Wendell Holmes, "It is November and the leaves that shelter my generation are falling fast." Then he went on to write, "Once our world was full of older men who were magnificent individuals in the grand manner. Many big oaks sheltered us. In this November, they fall fast, we are now our own front line."

A mighty oak has fallen. _____ was like a tree planted by a stream of water, which bore fruit at the right time, whose leaves did not wither and dry up. He was a mighty oak. [Enlarge here with a brief eulogy regarding his service, accomplishments, and so on.]

We all feel a profound loss. He worked for the "salvation of all mankind." He instructed us by precept and word to live self-controlled, upright, and godly lives in this world. His roots were deep. He stood uncompromisingly in the storms and struggles. We all felt secure and protected as long as he was on the scene. He has fallen and "we are now our own front line."

In the last sermon that Martin Luther King, Jr., preached at the Ebenezer Baptist Church in Atlanta, Georgia, he said, "If any of you are around when I have to meet my day, I don't want a long speech. I'd like somebody to mention that day that Martin Luther King, Jr., tried to give his life for others. I'd like somebody to say that day that Martin Luther King, Jr., tried to love somebody. I want you to say that day that I tried to be like and to walk with them. I won't have any money to leave behind. I won't have the fine and luxurious things of life to leave behind. But I just want to leave a committed life behind. Then my living will not be in vain."[1]

We remember _____ as one who gave his life for others, who loved people, and as one who was committed to public service. May the example of his life be emulated by us.

Hymn (optional)

"Lead On, O King Eternal"

Benediction

Now unto the King eternal, immortal, invisible, the only wise God, be honour and glory for ever and ever. Amen (1 Timothy 1:17).

Postlude

"Sunset and Evening Star"
"How Firm a Foundation"

26

FOR A MIDDLE-AGED PERSON

Prelude

"I Know Not What the Future Hath"
"O Love That Wilt Not Let Me Go"

Opening Sentence

The light of God surrounds us,
The love of God enfolds us,

The power of God protects us,
The presence of God is with us,
Wherever we are,
Wherever [name of deceased] is,
God is.[1]

Invocation

Almighty God, Father of mercies, and Giver of all comfort; deal graciously, we pray Thee, with all who mourn, that casting every care on Thee, they may know the consolation of Thy love and that Thou dost grant to the obedient and faithful an abundant entrance into Thy Kingdom, through Jesus Christ, our Lord. Amen.

Hymn (optional)

"Sunset and Evening Star"
"All Creatures of Our God and King"

Old Testament Scripture Readings

Psalms 24:3–5
Psalms 90:10
Isaiah 4:10, 28–31

New Testament Scripture Readings

Matthew 5:3–16
Luke 12:6, 7
2 Corinthians 1:3, 4
1 John 4:16–21

Brief Eulogy

[Briefly give factual information, characterization, and warm appreciation for the person's life.]

Pastoral Prayer

God of all life, we thank You for the one in whose memory we are met and for the seasons in which Your love and providence has blessed her life.

Thou hast provided the seed of life as men and angels united in singing and love. In the spring of glorious light, hearts have blossomed forth in all the purity, innocence, and simplicity of childhood.

In the summer, You revealed Yourself in the processions of earth's planted fields and heaven's sparkling light. From Thee have come health and growth and hope. The summer of youth with all of its beauty is a miracle wrought before our very eyes.

Dear God, how beautiful You have made the autumn season, with its glowing foliage and bountiful harvest. You have made humans beautiful in spirit, ever maturing after Your own image. We see Thy creative hand in all of life, especially when autumn leaves begin to fall.

O God of beauty, what white purity and gentle charity emerge with the chill of winter. In the winter of life, we are grateful that no winds or storms can make the sun to falter. How steadfast is Thy love; how constant is Thy truth, O God.

May life's end find us grateful and at peace with ourselves, our fellowmen, and with Thee, O God, through Jesus Christ. Amen.

Meditation

STRENGTH FOR YOUR HEART

An ancient songwriter captured something of the inner trauma, loneliness, shock, and despair that many of us feel. He shares with us the source of strength that sustained him and offers us good counsel. Listen to the Psalmist, "I had fainted, unless I had believed to see the goodness of the Lord in the land of the living. Wait on the Lord: be of good courage, and he shall strengthen thine heart: wait, I say, on the Lord" (Psalms 27:13, 14).

Do not expect healing from grief and fear instantly. Wait! God will provide.

We who were friends or working associates of _____ feel pangs of loneliness and emptiness since her death. A painful void has been left in our midst.

Each person will miss her in a different way. Those of the immediate family will experience the most profound loss. You may be out of town on business or on vacation. Then the realization will dawn that one of the persons who always has been interested in you and your doings will not be waiting anymore.

You may be browsing through a gift shop here or in faraway places, when you realize that one of the persons you always remembered with a gift does not need one anymore.

At a family gathering, you will suddenly realize that the firm voice that always got the grandchildren in line and called the clan to dinner will be silent.

Then there are those certain moments you do not think about now, but you will feel the pain when they happen. For instance when you receive some recognition or your picture is in the paper, the one who would be so proud of you, the one with whom you always shared your joys, the one who always was a source of encouragement will be gone. Or when a family member or relative faces a long illness, the one you have habitually depended upon for concern and strength is now absent. At joyous occasions such as birthdays, weddings, holidays there will be an empty chair for the one whom we admire and respect so much.

We would faint and collapse in despair were it not for our faith in the goodness of the Lord. More than the Psalmist have exclaimed, "What if I had not believed in the goodness of the Lord?" I could never have made it. My faith was my strength and my salvation!

So I say, "Wait for the Lord; take courage, and He will give strength to your heart."

This I Know
Grief has its rhythm—first, the
   Wild swift tide of dark despair;
The time of bleak aloneness
   When even God seems not there.

And then, the slow receding—
　　Till quiet calms the sea,
And bare, unwashed sand everywhere
　　Where castles used to be.

The gentle lapping of the waves
　　Upon the shore—and then,
The pearl lined shells of memories
　　To help us smile again.[2]

AUTHOR UNKNOWN

That which will do most to console our trembling heart is the hope in God's provisions for the future.

A minister took his five-year-old grandson on a stroll through the park. The little fellow carried on a running conversation of questions. He asked, "Gramps, why are those lines in your face? Why don't you have hair?" "I guess it means that I'm getting old," Gramps explained.

"Gramps, does everybody get lines and grow old?"

"Everybody gets old sooner or later, and that includes you."

"Gramps, what happens after you get old?"

"Well, in time you die."

"Do you think you will die, Gramps?"

"Oh, yes, everybody dies, and that includes me." After a long silence, the boy asked. "Gramps, will I get lines and lose my hair, and will I die?"

"Yes, Tad, you will get lines; you may not lose your hair; and someday, a long time from now, you will die."

"What happens then, Gramps?"

The grandfather believed it best to answer a child's questions directly, not to be evasive or untruthful. So he sat down with Tad and explained the best he could.

"Tad, the teeth you have now are called baby teeth. One of these years when they get loose and cannot chew food so well, they will come out. But second teeth will come in. Sometimes it is painful. So when a person's body grows old and cannot do its work, it is replaced by a second body."

While Gramps and his grandson were talking, a butterfly darted by, distracting Tad. "Gramps, where do butterflies come from?" Gramps explained, "In the park we have seen fuzzy little worms called caterpillars." "There is one in our backyard tree," Tad exclaimed. "When it becomes old enough, it lays aside its cocoon body and turns into a gorgeous multi-colored butterfly like this one. Isn't that marvelous?" Gramps continued.

"We, too, live in bodies until they grow lined and too sick to live in any longer. Through a dying process, according to the wisdom of God, we are transformed into glorified, spiritual bodies. That's what we believe, Tad."

Alice Freeman Palmer has put this faith in verse:

> I hold you at last in my hand,
> Exquisite child of the air.
> Can I ever understand
> How you grew to be so fair?
>
> Now I hold you fast in my hand,
> You marvelous butterfly,
> Till you help me to understand
> The eternal mystery.
>
> From that creeping thing in the dust
> To this shining bliss in the blue!
> God gives me courage to trust
> I can break my chrysalis too!

"Wait on the Lord: Be of good courage, and he shall strengthen thine heart. . . ."

Benediction

Clinging to the promise of Jesus, "I am the resurrection, and the life: he that believeth in me, though he were dead, yet shall he live" (John 11:25), we commit our loved one to Your keeping, O God, confident in Your wisdom, love, and everlastingness, through Jesus Christ, our Lord. Amen.

Postlude

"Blessed Assurance"
"God Will Take Care of You"

27

FOR A PERSON OF ANOTHER DENOMINATION

Prelude

"O Sacred Head, Now Wounded"

Opening Sentences

... How dreadful is this place! this is none other but the house of God, and this is the gate of heaven.

Genesis 28:17

Behold, how good and how pleasant it is for brethren to dwell together in unity! It is like the precious ointment upon the head ... As the dew of Hermon, and as the dew that descended upon the mountains of Zion. ...

Psalm 133

Invocation

Lord of life and love and beauty, help us to worship Thee in the beauty of holiness, that some beauty may be reflected in us. Quiet our souls before Thee with the stillness of a wise trust and a sense of being not in our hands, but in Thine. Lift us above the dark moods and the shadows, that we may begin today, from the height of prayer, to live as welcoming sons and daughters of the Most High. Amen.

Hymn (optional)

"O Lord Divine That Stooped to Share"

Old Testament Scripture Reading

General Selection:
   Psalm 121

Specifically Relevant Selections:

> O how love I thy law! it is my meditation all the
> day. . . . How sweet are thy words unto my taste! yea,
> sweeter than honey to my mouth! Through thy pre-
> cepts I get understanding: therefore I hate every false
> way. Thy word is a lamp unto my feet, and a light
> unto my path. I have sworn, and I will perform it,
> that I will keep thy righteous judgments. . . . Thy tes-
> timonies have I taken as an heritage for ever: for they
> are the rejoicing of my heart. I have inclined mine
> heart to perform thy statutes alway, even unto the
> end.
>
> Psalms 119:97, 103–106, 111, 112

> Seek ye the Lord while he may be found, call ye
> upon him while he is near; Let the wicked forsake his
> way, and the unrighteous man his thoughts: and let
> him return unto the Lord, and he will have mercy
> upon him; and to our God, for he will abundantly
> pardon. For my thoughts are not your thoughts, nei-
> ther are your ways my ways, saith the Lord. For as
> the heavens are higher than the earth, so are my ways
> higher than your ways, and my thoughts than your
> thoughts.
>
> Isaiah 55:6–9

New Testament Scripture Readings

General Selections:
   John 11:25, 26
   John 14:1–3

Specifically Relevant Selections:

> For I am not ashamed of the gospel of Christ: for it
> is the power of God unto salvation to every one that

believeth; to the Jew first, and also to the Greek. For therein is the righteousness of God revealed from faith to faith: as it is written, The just shall live by faith.

Romans 1:16, 17

There is one body, and one Spirit, even as ye are called in one hope of your calling; One Lord, one faith, one baptism, One God and Father of all, who is above all, and through all, and in you all.

Ephesians 4:4–6

Pastoral Prayer

God our Father, the support of those who put their trust in Thee, we turn to Thee in our sorrow. Even when we walk through the dark valley, You have promised us light to shine in our hearts, to guide us safely through the night of sorrow. Be Thou our friend, and we need ask no more in heaven or earth, for Thou art the comfort of all who trust Thee, the help and defense of all who hope in Thee.

O Lord, blend Thou our wills with Thine so we would have no fear of evil or death. We accept without murmur this separation knowing that Thou dost work in all things for good. Keep us ever in Thy love and truth, O Lord; comfort us with Thy light, and guide us by Thy Holy Spirit, through Jesus Christ, our Lord. Amen.

Hymn (optional)

"Come to Jesus, Ye Who Labor"

Meditation

HIS FACE BETRAYED THE SECRET

A most interesting story is associated with the founding of the Ancarda Mining Company in Montana. It all began when a group of prospectors set out for a place called Bannock, Montana, in search of gold. They were attacked by Indians, who took their horses. As the prospectors slowly worked their way back home, one of them picked up a stone from a creek bed, and it turned out to be gold. They decided among themselves that they would tell no one. They began to equip themselves with food and tools to return to search for the precious metal. When they were ready to go back, according to historical account, three hundred other prospectors followed them. No one had told them about the find, but they were highly suspicious. A reporter remarked, "Their beaming faces betrayed the secret."[1]

Jesus once made a comparable statement, "Ye shall know them by their fruits . . ." (Matthew 7:16). Ralph Waldo Emerson further elucidated, "Your actions speak so loudly, that I cannot hear what you say."

From the first time I met _____, until the last time, there was that smiling, beaming countenance which could not hide his love of people and his commitment to Jesus Christ. It stood out all over. There was always that radiance and glow. Though he became weak in body, he still had that "gleam in the eye" and jovial smile, indicating a strong spirit. He was not afraid of the future.

_____ was a member of another denomination than the one with which I am associated, yet because of my friendship, I was requested to share this memorial tribute with his church and community of friends. I am so glad to do so because he loved and served the same Lord whom I do. In Christ there is but one family, one body of people, one holy, universal church. All who love Christ are brothers and sisters in the faith. You will remember _____ for [enlarge with a brief personal characterization or eulogy]. It has been a joy to share _____'s life, family, faith, and home going.

A family moved to a new home. Unbeknown to the rest of the family, the mother planned a special surprise. She told the movers that when they unloaded the furniture she wanted everything in place just as it had been in their old home.

Not trusting their memories, the movers drew pictures of

each room before they moved a single piece of furniture. The mother showed them blueprints of her new home and discussed the adjustments they would have to make so things would fit.

Then while the movers did their work, the family took a leisurely trip to their new home. Two weeks later they drove up, walked through the front door, and discovered their mother's surprise. Although the two homes weren't exactly alike, the movers had done such a good job of placing the furniture that the family felt right at home in their new house.

Heaven will be like that. On the one hand, it will be filled with endless surprises. On the other, there will be so many things familiar to us that we will feel right at home.

Christ said: "For where your treasure is, there will your heart be also" (Matthew 6:21). Are you sending your treasures on ahead?

Benediction

Now to Him who is able to keep you from falling and to present you without blemish before the presence of His glory with rejoicing, to the only God, our Savior through Jesus Christ, our Lord, be glory, majesty, dominion, and authority before all time now and forever. Amen.

Postlude

"Holy Spirit, Faithful Guide"
"Ten Thousand Times Ten Thousand"

28

FOR AN UNSAVED PERSON

Prelude

"O God, Have Mercy," Bach

Opening Sentences

Let everyone be still, for God does not speak in audible words, but in meanings, in impressions, and in compulsions. Listen, that through the music, in the readings and prayers, through the spoken words and the beautiful atmosphere of this place, we may hear the still small voice of God—for God lights up people's hearts when they hear with the inner ear.

Invocation

Spirit of life, love, and beauty, indwelling all creation, who art the Person in all personhood and the good in all goodness, how majestic is Your name in all the universe. Not by logic but by intuition, not by fear but by love, not by power but by Spirit, not by chance but by Christ, we have come to know, to love, and to trust you, our Father and friend. Amen.

Old Testament Scripture Reading

General Selections:
Ecclesiastes 3:1–8
Psalms 24:3–5
Psalms 119:132–136

Specifically Relevant Selections:

I cried unto thee, O Lord: I said, Thou art my refuge and my portion in the land of the living. Attend unto my cry; for I am brought very low. . . . Bring my soul out of prison, that I may praise thy name: the righteous shall compass me about; for thou shalt deal bountifully with me.

Psalms 142:5–7

I will sing of the mercies of the Lord for ever: with my mouth will I make known thy faithfulness to all generations. For I have said, Mercy shall be built up for ever: thy faithfulness shalt thou establish in the very heavens. . . . And the heavens shall praise thy wonders, O Lord: thy faithfulness also in the congregation of the saints. For who in the heaven can be compared unto the Lord? who among the sons of the mighty can be likened unto the Lord? God is greatly to be feared in the assembly of the saints, and to be had in reverence of all them that are about him. O Lord God of hosts, who is a strong Lord like unto thee? or to thy faithfulness round about thee? Thou rulest the raging of the sea: when the waves thereof arise, thou stillest them. Thou hast broken Rahab in pieces, as one that is slain; thou hast scattered thine enemies with thy strong arm. The heavens are thine, the earth also is thine: as for the world and the fulness thereof, thou hast founded them. The north and the south thou hast created them: Tabor and Hermon shall rejoice in thy name. Thou hast a mighty arm: strong is thy hand, and high is thy right hand. Justice and judgment are the habitation of thy throne: mercy and truth shall go before thy face. Blessed is the people that know the joyful sound: they shall walk, O Lord, in the light of thy countenance. . . . Blessed be the lord for evermore. Amen, and Amen.

Psalms 89:1, 2, 5–15, 52

New Testament Scripture Readings

General Selection:
Philippians 4:7–16

Specifically Relevant Selections:

I thank my God, making mention of thee always in my prayers, Hearing of thy love and faith, which thou hast toward the Lord Jesus, and toward all the saints.

Philemon 4, 5

And he spake this parable unto certain which trusted in themselves that they were righteous, and despised others: Two men went up into the temple to pray; the one a Pharisee, and the other a publican. The Pharisee stood and prayed thus with himself, God, I thank thee, that I am not as other men are, extortioners, unjust, adulterers, or even as this publican. I fast twice in the week, I give tithes of all that I possess. And the publican, standing afar off, would not lift up so much as his eyes unto heaven, but smote upon his breast, saying, God be merciful to me a sinner. I tell you, this man went down to his house justified rather than the other: for every one that exalteth himself shall be abased; and he that humbleth himself shall be exalted.

Luke 18:9–14

That if thou shalt confess with thy mouth the Lord Jesus, and shalt believe in thine heart that God hath raised him from the dead, thou shalt be saved. For with the heart man believeth unto righteousness; and with the mouth confession is made unto salvation. For the scripture saith, Whosoever believeth on him shall not be ashamed. For there is no difference between the Jew and the Greek: for the same Lord over all is rich unto all that call upon him. For whosoever shall call upon the name of the Lord shall be saved.

Romans 10:9–13

Pastoral Prayer

Eternal God, from whom we have come, to whom we return, before whose face pass all the generations, in whose wisdom and mercy is our future, we bow before Thy greatness.

We thank Thee for the life of the one in whose memory we are met. Reward his goodness, be merciful with his shortcomings. We commit him to Thy care and take to heart the solemn responsibilities of living in union with Jesus Christ, the Savior and Redeemer. Amen.

Meditation

TRUSTING GOD'S CHARACTER

Carl Jung, the famous Swiss psychologist, once said, "Commendation heals; condemnation destroys."

At the outset, let us remember that it is not our prerogative to make ecclesiastical pronouncements about another person's destiny. Such alone is God's prerogative. No man is the Eternal Judge, however well he may know the Bible or the message of the Father or the individual. God alone knows the complete background, motives, and influences that are unique to an individual. So we never fall into the temptation of judging God or others.

Not much good is ever done by condemning even what we know is wrong, if by so doing a gulf is opened between the condemner and the condemned. We are not to condone evil, but we are to separate it from the one who does it and try to understand. If we knew all that God knows, only then could we be a judge.

So, in facing this loss, be glad for the good times that you have enjoyed with _____. Be appreciative of the many good qualities of his character, and the good deeds he rendered. Be thoughtful for the memories which linger.

Let us also meditate upon the character of God as the Psalmist knew him (Psalms 89:1, 2). The Psalmist had a difficult time understanding what God was doing, yet he knew God better than to doubt His goodness. In Genesis 18:25 we read, "Shall not the Judge of all the earth do right?" God is too good to be unkind and too wise to make mistakes. He is always trustworthy.

Anytime we are perplexed, we can trust God totally to do what is right. Righteousness and justice are the foundations of His theme. Reliability and faithfulness go before us. By meditating upon God's righteous goodness and faithfulness, we can put aside our fears and doubts. We can trust Him.

We can do nothing now for the dead. However we can minister to the needs of the living. We can be a testimony to God's grace and work in time of perplexity. We can grasp the opportunity to share the good news of salvation.

Remember, God never changes. If we can trust Him implicitly to meet our needs on earth, can we not trust Him now to meet our needs in the present and our loved one's needs in the future?

Crossing the Bar

Sunset and evening star,
    And one clear call for me!
And may there be no moaning at the bar,
    When I put out to sea.

But such a tide as moving seems asleep,
    Too full for sound and foam,
When that which drew from out the boundless deep,
    Turns again home.

Twilight and evening bell,
    And after that the dark!
And may there be no sadness of farewell,
    When I embark.

For though from out our bourne of Time and Place
    The flood may bear me far,
I hope to see my Pilot face to face
    When I have crossed the bar.

ALFRED TENNYSON

Benediction

God be merciful unto us, and bless us; and cause his face to shine upon us. That thy way may be known upon earth, thy saving health among all nations.

Psalms 67:1, 2

Postlude

"O World, I Now Must Leave Thee," Brahms

29

FOR AN INDIGENT PERSON

Prelude

"Come, Ye Disconsolate"
"What a Friend We Have in Jesus"
"The Love of God"

Opening Sentences

If thou, Lord, shouldest mark iniquities, O Lord, who shall stand? But there is forgiveness with thee . . . I wait for the Lord, my soul doth wait, and in his word do I hope . . . for with the Lord there is mercy, and with him is plenteous redemption. And he shall redeem Israel from all his iniquities.

Psalms 130:3–5, 7, 8

Invocation

O Thou who lovest us as though there were but one to love, who regards each one as precious, without qualification or deserving, minister to our minds and hearts, through Thy Holy Spirit, in Jesus Christ. Amen.

Hymn (optional)

"Jesus, Lover of My Soul"
"Amazing Grace"

Old Testament Scripture Readings

General Selections:
Psalm 130
Psalms 8:3–8

Specifically Relevant Selections:

And God said, Let us make man in our image,
after our likeness: and let them have dominion over
the fish of the sea, and over the fowl of the air, and
over the cattle, and over all the earth, and over every
creeping thing that creepeth upon the earth. So God
created man in his own image, in the image of God
created he him; male and female created he them.

Genesis 1:26, 27

Better it is to be of an humble spirit with the lowly,
than to divide the spoil with the proud. . . . The hoary
head is a crown of glory, if it be found in the way of
righteousness. He that is slow to anger is better than
the mighty; and he that ruleth his spirit than he that
taketh a city.

Proverbs 16:19, 31, 32

New Testament Scripture Readings

General Selection:
Luke 12:6, 7

Specifically Relevant Selection:

Put on therefore, as the elect of God . . . bowels of
mercies, kindness. . . . Forbearing one another, and

forgiving one another ... even as Christ forgave you. ...

Colossians 3:12, 13

Pastoral Prayer

Dear God, we are encouraged with the assurance that no one is ever beyond Your love and care. Though we categorize people into desirable and undesirable, good and bad, every person is of worth to You. Every person is precious and loved by You. We remember how Jesus loved the unlovely, ate with the publicans, helped the poor and forgave sinners.

We commend this brother to Your keeping. In the presence of Your love that will not let him go, may his potential blossom and his soul be reclaimed through the eternity of your grace and mercy, in Jesus' Spirit. Amen.

Meditation

THE DIGNITY OF BEING HUMAN

When the call came notifying me of _____'s death and requesting that I conduct the funeral, I was preparing a sermon on "The Dignity of Being a Member of the Human Race." There are all kinds of human beings, some better than others, some good, some bad. Some have been by birth more fortunate than others. Some have developed their God endowed abilities with greater diligence than others.

In any case, the truth remains that it is a great and unique privilege to be a human being. Every person has incalculable worth, by virtue of being a human. That is true of the person in whose memory we are gathered today.

The Psalmist long ago, while in reflective thought, asked God, the Creator, "When I consider thy heavens, the work of thy fingers, the moon and the stars, which thou hast ordained; What is man, that thou art mindful of him? . . . For thou hast made him a little lower than the angels. . . . Thou madest him to have dominion over the works of thy hands; thou hast put all things under his feet: All sheep and oxen, yea, and the beasts of the field; The fowl of the air, and the fish of the sea, and whatsoever passeth through the paths of the seas" (Psalms 8:3–8). To be a human being is to be set apart as God's supreme creation. As wondrous and majestic and vast as is all the rest, man is the greatest. Man is kin to the animal kingdom through his body and yet is uniquely different, a bit less than God Himself, containing the image of God, with abilities of thought, memory projection, and communication.

What is the part of us above the animal level? Well, the image of God in us permits us to say no to instincts on moral grounds. The whole story of being human is the story of rising above our animal natures and learning to control our instincts.

We have two dear family pets named Bengie and Lovey. They had puppies because with animals it is natural and non-problematic. With humans it should mean tenderness, sharing of affection, and responsible commitment, unless we just behave like animals. Our dog, Lovey, nursed her puppies as a purely instinctive process. When they were old enough to take care of themselves, she began to ignore them. Now, when Bengie, the father, meets Missy, his grown-up daughter, he recognizes another dog, not necessarily his own kin. Being a human parent is not that easy. Raising and teaching children, passing on your own values to them, sharing their hurts, knowing when to be tough and when to be forgiving—that is the painful part of your parenting. Human beings have to make choices between good and bad. The freedom to make the choice is the legacy of the human being!

Dignity is every person's birthright because every person possesses a freedom of choice, self-consciousness, thoughtful creativity, moral judgment, intelligent mind, self-understanding, and personality. There is much more to man than mere physical characteristics. There is spirit—the very stamp of our creation.

God dignified humanity by becoming enfleshed as we are, in Jesus Christ. Jesus simplified human value by His words, "Are not two sparrows sold for a farthing? and one of them shall not fall on the ground without your Father.... ye are of much more value than many sparrows" (Matthew 10:29, 31). That says something about the greatness and omniscience of God. However, it says much about the great value God places upon the human being.

God's love was revealed in the self-sacrificing of Jesus dying upon the cross for the salvation of His children. "Greater love hath no man than this, that a man lay down his life for his friends" (John 15:13). No person for whom Christ died can ever be considered worthless, insignificant, or of no value.

So we witness today to the value of every human being, not the least of whom is _____.

But "who is _____ that God and we should be mindful of him?" (*See* Psalms 8:4).

This we affirm about _____ and every human: The real value roots in being God's child. God is "our Father." We all belong to the human family. We all have the same father; therefore, we are all brothers and sisters. No person can ever be to us an enemy or an object of discrimination or scorn.

Our society too much determines human worth in terms of property or possessions accumulated. Worth is bound up with culture, education, money, talent, position, even race or social rank. When a person loses his job or mechanization replaces him, or one does not succeed in becoming wealthy, he is considered of less worth. When age takes away beauty, when jobs are denied in favor of the younger and better educated—then self-esteem and a feeling of importance may crumble. If the community says that being black is bad, Mexican is undesirable, Indian is evil, and poor is scornful, we betray the one basis of human worth.

We are next of kin to God—every one of us. God is our nearest relative.

Our brother has died. He is precious to our Father. Therefore, he is precious to us. To God we commit his keeping.

Hymn (optional)

"His Eye Is on the Sparrow"

Benediction

We go forth with head up, standing on tiptoe, feeling good and self-confident because of Your love for us, O God. May the imprint of that love be manifest in all that we do forever and ever. Amen.

Postlude

"My Hope Is Built on Nothing Less"
"Jesus, Friend of Sinners," Grieg

30

FOR A GRANDPARENT

Prelude

"Near to the Heart of God"
"Blessed Assurance"

Opening Sentences

Dear friends, never forget that "after the night comes a new day, after the winter another spring, after the storm a sun-drenched earth, after sin comes forgiveness, after defeat comes another chance."[1] After death is heaven.

Let us pray:

Invocation

God and Father, the hiding place from the wind and a shelter from the storms, we turn from the distress and despair of the world to the calm of Thy great assurance, through Jesus Christ, our Lord. Amen.

For a Grandparent

Hymn (optional)

"Still, Still With Thee"

Old Testament Scripture Reading

General Selection:
Psalm 23

Specifically Relevant Selection:

> And these words, which I command thee this day, shall be in thine heart: And thou shalt teach them diligently unto thy children, and shalt talk of them when thou sittest in thine house, and when thou walkest by the way, and when thou liest down, and when thou risest up. And thou shalt bind them for a sign upon thine hand, and they shall be as frontlets between thine eyes. And thou shalt write them upon the posts of thy house, and on thy gates.
> Deuteronomy 6:6–9

New Testament Reading

General Selection:
John 14:1–3, 27

Specifically Relevant Selection:

> Wherefore seeing we also are compassed about with so great a cloud of witnesses, let us lay aside every weight, and the sin which doth so easily beset us, and let us run with patience the race that is set before us, Looking unto Jesus the author and finisher of our faith; who for the joy that was set before him endured the cross, despising the shame, and is set down at the right hand of the throne of God.
> Hebrews 12:1, 2

Pastoral Prayer

Our heavenly Father, to whom we turn in every time of darkness to pour out our griefs to Thee and to rest our troubled hearts under the shelter of Thy love, hear now our prayer for those who are bowed down in sorrow and affliction. In their darkness, may Thy light shine. In their loneliness, may Thy presence be felt. Thou hast given assurance that death is but a gate of entrance to another world of life.

O Father of comfort, grant to these, in their time of bereavement, the joy and consolation of hope that when we part from those taken away by death, we may say in our hearts that we shall meet again. May we who remain behind keep ever clear and bright the memory of their lives. May we be blessed even now by a true communion of spirit with the unseen world and live as members of one family on earth and in heaven, in Jesus' name. Amen.

Hymn (optional)

"Open the Gates of the Temple"
"How Beautiful Upon the Mountain"

Meditation

"LISTEN! YOUR GRANDPARENT IS SPEAKING"

Our lives are like a pebble tossed into a pond, leaving ever-widening rings and ripples of influence. Long after a stone disappears, the ripples continue.

Just so, after a person passes from our sight, the impact of his knowledge, values, sacrifices, faith live on in the membership of family love. That is why we are here today—to lift up in our memory _____, the appreciation for his struggles, character, and life, remembering what is true, just, honorable, pure, lovely, gracious and excellent.

Ever since Alex Haley's book and subsequent film entitled, *Roots,* it has been popular to look back to one's heritage, to those who have gone before us, to reconstruct their trials, victories, defeats, and deprivations endured, to view their hopes and dreams. We have come here to do that as children, grandchildren, great-grandchildren, and friends. Margaret Mead, the anthropologist, says we need to do it. In turbulent changes, people often feel restless and rootless. The best antidote is to see how our elders coped with upheaval. She says that our stability, sense of continuity, and society depend upon it.

The Rotary magazine recently carried an article entitled, "Listen, Your Grandfather Is Speaking!" We would not let _____ fade from our memory without this penetrating moment when deep calls to deep and we listen to what _____ is saying to us. He is saying something about values [enlarge here]. By his example, your grandfather is saying something about the importance of service to your fellowmen [enlarge]. Listen—your grandparents are speaking! What do you hear? This is the way faith and hope and love are transmitted from generation to generation. In Deuteronomy 6:6–9 Moses advised the Israelites. "And these words, which I command thee this day, shall be in thine heart: And thou shalt teach them diligently unto thy children, and shalt talk of them when thou sittest in thine house, and when thou walkest by the way, and when thou liest down, and when thou risest up. And thou shalt bind them for a sign upon thine hand, and they shall be as frontlets between thine eyes. And thou shalt write them upon the posts of thy house, and on thy gates."

Sometime ago, an eighty-year-old grandfather died. One of his sons wrote a tribute:

> Recently, as the Lord was going about seeking citizens for His Kingdom, He was asked by an angel, "Have you considered my servant Fay Smith? He is a just and upright man, who fears and serves God. His life has been productive and useful, because his life has been motivated by Christ's Spirit. . . . He has produced fruits such as love, joy, peace, and many others . . . his life has not been an easy road. No, not at all. His faith has been tested by flood and hail, by failure and the depression. But by all these things his faith was truly strengthened because he knew that the

things of this life are only temporary. While you are considering, consider his wife of more than half a century. She, too loved God and has been Fay's right hand!"

The Lord listened intently, then said, "It is time for me to call him home and give him his full reward, but his wife's time has not yet come. I still have things for her to do, lives to touch and love to share."[2]

Life is like a relay race, where the baton of values, character, and faith are passed from one generation to another. The runner ahead passes it on, runs by our side for a while, and then we pass it on to those who come after us, one by one.

In 1948 at the Olympic games, the French relay team was well ahead. The first two runners had been amazingly swift. But when the second runner passed the baton to the third runner, it was dropped. What a moment of tragedy. The nation's hopes were shattered. The coaches' work went for naught. The first two runners' performances were all in vain. The fourth runner did not have a chance. The boy who dropped the baton fell down and wept.

Your family continuity is in balance. The baton of one generation's values and faith is being passed on. Don't drop the baton. "Listen, your grandfather is speaking."

"Speak . . . for your servant hears."

Benediction

"The Lord bless thee, and keep thee: the Lord make his face shine upon thee, and be gracious unto thee: the Lord lift up his countenance upon thee, and give thee peace" (Numbers 6:24–26), in your going out and your coming in, in your lying down and your rising up, in your labor and your leisure, in your laughter and in your tears, until you come to stand before Jesus in the day in which there is no sunset and no dawning. Amen.

Postlude

"Sunset and Evening Star"

31

FOR AN ATHLETE

Prelude

"Immortal, Invisible, God Only Wise"
"O Christ, the Way, the Truth, the Life"

Opening Sentences

For everything its season, and for every activity
under heaven its time:
a time to be born and a time to die;
a time to plant and a time to uproot; ...
a time to weep and a time to laugh;
a time for mourning and a time for dancing; ...
a time to seek and a time to lose;
a time to keep and a time to throw away; ...
a time for silence and a time for speech;
a time to love ... a time for peace.
Ecclesiastes 3:1–4, 6–8 NEB

Invocation

Our good Father, we thank Thee for all the beneficial times
and seasons of life—the beauty of the spring of our life, the
fruitfulness of our summer, the glory of our autumn, and comfort and faith in winter. We thank Thee for Thy loving care in
every season and the appropriate timing for all things. May we
accept without regret the death this time has brought. Admit
him, we pray, into the richer life of heaven, in Jesus' name.
Amen.

Hymn (optional)

"Fairest Lord Jesus"

Old Testament Scripture Readings

General Selections:
Psalms 42:1, 2, 11
Psalms 90:1–8, 10, 16, 17
Isaiah 40:31
Isaiah 41:10, 13

New Testament Scripture Readings

General Selections:
Hebrews 12:1, 2
Romans 8:35, 37–39
2 Corinthians 5:1
Ephesians 6:10–18
2 Timothy 4: 6–8

Pastoral Prayer

Eternal Spirit, Father of our spirits, in whose fellowship is our peace, we turn our trust to Thee. Amid these moments that have shaken us emotionally, remind us of all the assets and joys that have blessed our lives in these years.

We thank You, dear God, for the cherished memories of _____ which shall be forever written upon the canvas of our minds, for his goodness, his abilities, his dedication to Christ and the church, his love of family, his joy of life, his unselfish service. He has been taken from our midst, to live and love with You.

God eternal, grant us Your perspective, we pray: It is not how long we live that counts; it is how meaningfully we live that matters. It is not the duration that adds significance; it is the devotion of life that does. Heavenly Father, we remember Your own Son, who died at thirty-three years of age, but who outlived, outloved, and outdied everyone. From the inspiration and example of Jesus, our elder brother, help us to live more dedicated lives that will justify the longer years Your providence gives us.

Gracious Father, relieve with the assurance of Your forgiveness, the feelings of guilt and remorse for what we did or did not do. Help this family through its sorrow, so their home will not be a shrine of grief. Help them to assimilate the loss and to live for the future, deepened in faith, enriched by _____'s influence, sustained by the bonds of Christ's love, at peace with You, constant in service and ready for their summons to the higher and more blessed life, through Jesus Christ. Amen.

Meditation

THE SEASONS OF LIFE

There is a book entitled *The Seasons of a Man's Life,* which is suggestive for our meditation today.

When we think of _____'s life, at the outset we think of the athletic seasons. He was a versatile, accomplished, and well-known athlete. What thrilling moments he has brought to so many fans. He was a man's man for all seasons.

I think of him in the baseball season, during which he [enlarge on his attainment]. During the basketball season we, who were rabid basketball fans, have been caught up in his ability to put his team in the lead or to come from behind. Perhaps the greatest thrills have come in the "football season" as _____ has excelled in passing, running, and kicking. He was known as a "triple threat." We mourn his death, for truly he was an athlete for all seasons and of all sports. With his fine physique, quick reflexes, heady play, and competitive spirit, he was the idol of many young boys and girls, as well as sports fans throughout the area.

A person's life can also be thought in terms of other seasons of the year, the spring of childhood, the summer of youth, the autumn of maturity, finally the winter of old age. [Here the minister may give interesting facts about birth and childhood (the spring of life); of his youth, education, and so on (the summer of life); of his marriage, family, occupation, and church (the autumn of life); then finally the frosty winters (if he reached old age)].

Look at the seasons:

The spring of the year! The world is a poem of light and color. The meadow is green and turns somersaults of joy. All the butterflies flutter from the buttercups. And it is beautiful. But it does not stay long.

It gets hot, everything turns brown. The grasshopper drags himself along. Cracks appear in the parched earth. Those heat waves come up from the highway and railroad. And everybody is tinkering with the air conditioning. But it does not last long.

The cool breezes blow and the school bell rings and leaves turn to flame. The days grow short; the football is kicked into the air, and the referee blows the whistle. It's the fall of the year. But not for long.

For the leaves are bitten from the trees and piled in a heap against the back fence. And the bony, naked fingers of the trees pray for cover now. Then down from God's mercy comes a blanket of snow. And the flying cloud and the frosty light, and the year's dying in the night, and someone says "Happy New Year!"[1]

I like to think that life is a year we spend on earth, with its varied terrain, beauty, and unique joys and opportunities. Not all the years are the same. Some are filled with extremes of cold or heat. Some are good economically; others are filled with reversals. Each of us spends a year in the park. Some live only through the springtime before being called away; others enjoy the thrill and pleasure of youth's summer. Still others are privileged to see the turning of the trees, to smell new-mown hay, and to watch autumn's fallen leaves. Still others stay until the white snow covers the earth, as winter's icy fingers feebly reach out. For each of us comes the time when the nurse, death, takes us by the hand. To our friend, death came at the noon of day, in the summer of youth [or whatever the season].

The Indian poet, Nancy Wood has written:

> I remember you when
> The humming insects mother
> The newborn leaves of spring.
> I remember you when
> The arguments of frogs becomes
> The laughing song of summer.
> I remember you when
> I hear my corn begin to grow
> And beauty crowds my life.
> I remember you when
> The tame rose sleeps
> Between the jaws of winter.
> Here I am in the winter of my years
> Having lived with you since spring, and yet
> Where did autumn go?[2]

It was said on the occasion of Senator Sam Rayburn's death, "It is November and the leaves that shelter my generation are falling fast."

The good news is that there is a man for all your seasons of life. A man who meets all the needs of all ages. His name is Jesus Christ. He died as the autumn leaves began to fall. He was vindicated by God in resurrection. His Spirit lives on. He will never be forgotten. He said, "Because I live, you shall live." This is your man for all your seasons, who gives you life forever and ever.

Hymn (optional)

"O Master Let Me Walk With Thee"

Benediction

I have fought a good fight, I have finished my course, I have kept the faith: Henceforth there is laid up for me a crown of righteousness, which the Lord, the righteous judge, shall give me at that day: and not to me only, but unto all them also that love his appearing.

2 Timothy 4:7, 8

Postlude

"Holy Spirit, Faithful Guide"

32

FOR A LINGERING DEATH

Prelude

"My Faith Looks Up to Thee"
"O Sacred Head, Now Wounded"

Opening Sentences

Death is not extinguishing the light. It is putting out the lamp because the dawn has come. "The Lord is my light and my salvation; whom shall I fear?" (Psalms 27:1 RSV).

Invocation

Eternal Source of Life, the Light of every mind that knows Thee and the Hope of every soul that loves Thee, from our earthly view we would move into Thy larger perspective; from lingering suffering we would find Thy great release; from this temporal life we would take hold of eternal life, with Jesus Christ our good Physician. Amen.

Old Testament Scripture Readings

General Selections:
    Psalms 46:1–3
    2 Samuel 22:2, 3

Specifically Relevant Selection:

> Lord, my heart is not haughty, nor mine eyes lofty: neither do I exercise myself in great matters, or in things too high for me. Surely I have behaved and quieted myself, as a child that is weaned of his mother: my soul is even as a weaned child. Let Israel hope in the Lord from henceforth and for ever.

Psalm 131

New Testament Scripture Readings

General Selections:
 Romans 8:31–34
 Romans 8:35, 37–39

Specifically Relevant Selections:

> For our light affliction, which is but for a moment, worketh for us a far more exceeding and eternal weight of glory; While we look not at the things which are seen, but at the things which are not seen: for the things which are seen are temporal; but the things which are not seen are eternal.

2 Corinthians 4:17, 18

> They shall hunger no more, neither thirst any more; neither shall the sun light on them, nor any heat. For the Lamb which is in the midst of the throne shall feed them, and shall lead them unto living fountains of waters: and God shall wipe away all tears from their eyes.

Revelation 7:16, 17

> And God shall wipe away all tears from their eyes; and there shall be no more death, neither sorrow, nor crying, neither shall there be any more pain; for the former things are passed away.

Revelation 21:4

Pastoral Prayer

God and Lord of all worlds, seen and unseen, transient and eternal, Creator of our bodies, Father of our spirits, we turn to Thee.

Thou hast so mysteriously made us that, living in the midst of the temporal, we think thoughts of eternity. Thy promises are written in our hearts; we believe them. What eye has not seen, nor ear heard, and what has not entered into the hearts of man, you have laid up for them that love Thee. Give us eyes to see the open road ahead, and touch our spirits with Thy radiant hope.

Give us the sense of the Easter victory that turned a cross into a resurrection and made the one-time symbol of shame the sign of spiritual triumph that turned death into life, that transformed tragedy into faith and all bitterness into love. So may it touch our hearts today, through Jesus Christ our Lord. Amen.

Hymn (optional)

"In the Hour of Trial"
"In the Cross of Christ I Glory"
"God's Tomorrow"
"Sunrise Tomorrow"

Meditation

GROWING INWARDLY ON THE WAY TO DEATH

_____ whom we honor today was one who has faced a long and lingering death. Many of us can scarcely remember him when he was not ill. In the latter months he has endured excruciating pain, as those of us who have known him can affirm, yet he did so courageously, without complaining, as though he had an unlimited source of power or a transcendent spirit that paid no attention to pain. What an inspiration.

He has made believable the affirmation of Paul written to

the Corinthians, ". . . Though our outward man perish, yet the inward man is renewed day by day" (2 Corinthians 4:16).

I have known many people who have suffered physically. Understandably many have wallowed in self-pity, resentment, and bitterness. The struggle made them unpleasant, contentious, and habitual complainers. They deteriorated inwardly even as they wasted away outwardly.

The Apostle Paul says that there is a faith that helps one to take the suffering as a part of life. If we cannot find healing and comfort, we can find resources in Christ to take it graciously and to stop resenting and resisting it. Once a person can do that, he grows inwardly on his way to death. One may wither away physically as age or disease take its toll, yet by reaching up to God and out to others, a miracle takes place—inward renewal.

This is the power of the cross. I have been studying the words of Jesus from the cross, as He lingered, life ebbing away. As far as I can tell from the gospels, Jesus was a stranger to personal physical suffering, until the cross. Though He spent much time among the suffering and serving them, yet there is no reference that He was ever sick. He did not have tuberculosis, like Robert Louis Stevenson, or cancer, as did Dr. Tom Dooley, or asthma, as a friend of mine. He was not deaf, like Beethoven. He had no emotional disorders or long depressions, as did theologian Don Baillie. There is no sign that He was hungry, except when He fasted and was tempted in the wilderness. But when He was crucified, Jesus suffered terribly— excruciating, lingering, agonizing pain. It was a slow death incomprehensible to our sensibilities. He suffered, but He did it magnificently. His great spirit held up; His faith did not fluctuate. We admire the nobleness of His spirit in death. He was renewed inwardly, which must have inspired our dear friend. May we be renewed inwardly as well, so that as life fades away, we may have resources to meet what we must.

Benediction

Eternal Father, by Thy goodness we have been brought to the evening of this life, in peace; we feel Thee to be near; we know Thee to be good; we trust Thee. Now may the angel of Thy peace go before us until we come to Thy holy hill, where our rest and Thine honor dwell, world without end, through Jesus Christ. Amen.

Postlude

"Still, Still With Thee"
"Now the Day Is Over"

33

FOR ALMOST ANYONE

Prelude

"All Creatures of Our God and King"
"Thou Wilt Keep Him"

Opening Sentences

We come here today:

As a soul standing in awe before the mystery of the universe.
As a poet enthralled with the beauty of a sunrise,
As a person listening through a tornado for the still small voice,
As a drop of water in quest of the ocean,
As a workman pausing to listen to a beautiful strain of music,
As a Prodigal running to his Father,
As Time flowing into Eternity,
As a child climbing into the lap of his father.[1]

Come, let us pray:

Invocation

Soul of the universe, the essence of personality, the center of consciousness, the energizer of life and infinitely more, we bow in awe and humility, trusting that there is more to life than is confined to the body and more to existence than death can give. We commit the future to you, Lord Jesus. Amen.

Hymn (optional)

"How Firm a Foundation"

Old Testament Scripture Readings

General Selections:
  Psalms 46:1–5
  Psalms 90:10, 12, 16, 17
  Psalm 1

Specifically Relevant Selection:

> As the hart panteth after the water brooks, so panteth my soul after thee, O God. My soul thirsteth for God, for the living God: when shall I come and appear before God? . . . Why art thou cast down, O my soul? and why art thou disquieted within me? hope thou in God: for I shall yet praise him, who is the health of my countenance, and my God.
>
> Psalms 42:1, 2, 11

New Testament Scripture Readings

General Selections:
  Matthew 5:3–12
  Matthew 6:19–21
  Matthew 7:24–27
  John 14:27
  Titus 2:11–14

Pastoral Prayer

Eternal God, Lord of Life, and Conqueror of death, help us
to know that we are spiritual beings living in a spiritual universe, so we need not fear death. Help us to believe that, while
the things that are seen, pass away and the things that are unseen are real and eternal, so we need not despair. Help us to
realize that death cannot take away or destroy the soul recon-
ciled in Christ, so we can by grace be at peace.

Help us to cherish the precious memories that enfold the life
we have loved so that we may be humbled in gratitude and inspired to emulate what is good and fine, through Jesus Christ,
our Lord. Amen.

Meditation

WHY WE ARE HERE

A funeral service has several significant purposes.

First, it is a *memorial* service. We are here to remember our
mutual friend _____. A generation ago the seminary theologi-
cal departments were advocating formal, standardized funeral
services. A minister was urged to use the prayer book with the
same Scriptures, verses, prayers, and hymns for all persons.
Also he should not mention the deceased by name or give personal references.

Today, however, it is generally felt appropriate to make the
service personal, not necessarily to give a eulogy or exagger-
ated assessment or to give ecclesiastical judgments; nonetheless,
it is comforting to give some sort of mutual appreciation for the
person's life and a characterization of personality. So we have
come here today to remember the good qualities of _____.
[Minister should include here a brief talk about the person
honored.]

Someone said, "I want to die young, but as late in life as
possible." The person we honor was young in spirit and is remembered with appreciation.

Also this is a *service* of healing. The grief syndrome inevita-
bly takes a person emotionally through the journey of disbe-

lief, rebellion, numbness, anger, loneliness, hostility, guilt, and finally to acceptance and assimilation. For some the healing is more rapid than for others. Not always are the feelings in the same sequence. Nevertheless, the process has to be faced, and each emotion has to be dealt with satisfactorily.

The funeral service is designed so the reality of death is faced; the family and friends become a shield of love; it provides an atmosphere for recalling and weeping. Pastoral prayers for forgiveness, intercessions, and petitions for strength are rendered. Biblical assurances are read. The Holy Spirit, the Comforter, brings the "peace that passes all understanding." There is healing in faith, hope, and love.

One popular song confirms a very great truth: People need people, especially at the time of sorrow. People are a source of healing.

Finally, the funeral is a *celebration* service of reaffirming faith in God and Eternal Life. A man whose son died of cancer said it this way, "I do not know how people can face death without God. I know I could not."

Several years ago a man took his new outboard motor boat to Yellowtail Reservoir in Northern Wyoming, not far from the scenes of Custer's Last Stand. The boat he bought had styrofoam floats so it could not sink. He insisted upon this security, he said, "So the fear of capsizing would not destroy the joy of the family outings."

One afternoon while they were on the lake, a fierce storm suddenly arose as it frequently does in that north country, causing huge whitecaps that totally filled the boat. The boat sank to the level of the top. A companion in another boat yelled, "Look out! Your boat may sink!" "I have floats in it," replied the man. "I don't want to see it go down. I don't anticipate that it will. We have life preservers on, furthermore I can swim. I am not afraid!"

We cannot enjoy living until we have settled the issue of death! Don't you know that at any moment that body of yours may fall into disrepair or be overcome by accident or crumble with age?

"Oh, yes, I do," is the reply. "Let it go when it must, but remember I have a faith that buoys me up, and I can swim."

This is the promise of our Lord, "When thou passest through the waters, I will be with thee; and through the rivers, they shall not overflow thee.... For I am the Lord thy God ..." (Isaiah 43:2, 3). "... Nay, in all these things we are more than conquerors through him that loved us" (Romans 8:37). "... God is our refuge and strength, a very present help in trouble" (Psalms 46:1). Therefore, we will not fear!

A handsome young husband lost his wife. A great shadow of despair hung over his soul. At the funeral, the minister prayed silently for him.

After the service, the grief-stricken husband stood alone at the casket with the minister near. Then the miracle happened. Looking up with a tearful face he prayed, "Lord, I give her back to you." He stood tall and straight again. As he regained composure, he looked at his minister and said, "She is in God's hands now." He walked strongly away. He had surrendered her to God. He found the faith to move the mountain of grief. And the sunshine of warm peace fell into his mind.[2]

Hymn (optional)

"O Jesus, I Have Promised"
"Beyond the Sunset"

Benediction

O God
in all this confusion
you're the only one
That's real.

You're my foundation.
On you I can depend
In you I find
Peace
Strength
Truth
and Beauty

24:00

In you
I can go on
No matter what the future holds,
For you have
Past
Present
Future
In your hands

I can unload my pain now,
And depend upon you.
I can trust myself
and the future.
Thank you.

I'm not afraid of the
future now, God.
In fact, I might even enjoy it.[3]

Postlude

"Blest Be the Tie"
"Thine Be the Glory"

34

FOR AN AGED SHUT-IN

Prelude

"Near to the Heart of God"

Opening Sentences

". . . Weeping may endure for the night, but joy cometh in the morning" (Psalms 30:5). "For God hath not given us the spirit of fear; but of power, and of love, and of a sound mind" (2 Timothy 1:7).

Invocation

Heavenly Father, there is much to be thankful for today. This mother lived long enough to be known by grandchildren and great-grandchildren, sharing her faith, wisdom, values, and character. We are thankful for the release that death has brought and for the promise of an eternal home. We thank You, Father God, for the promise to be a constant heavenly Parent and the assurance that though "weeping may endure for the night, . . . joy comes in the morning," in Jesus' name. Amen.

Old Testament Scripture Readings

General Selections:
  Ecclesiastes 3:1–8, 10, 11
  Psalm 121

Specifically Relevant Selection:

> The days of our years are threescore years and ten; and if by reason of strength they be fourscore years, yet is their strength labour and sorrow; for it is soon cut off, and we fly away. . . . So teach us to number our days, that we may apply our hearts unto wisdom. . . . Let thy work appear unto thy servants, and thy glory unto their children. And let the beauty of the Lord our God be upon us: and establish thou the work of our hands upon us; yea, the work of our hands establish thou it.
>
> Psalms 90:10, 12, 16, 17

New Testament Scripture Readings

General Selections:
  John 11:25, 26
  John 14:1–3

Specifically Relevant Selection:

> For this corruptible must put on incorruption, and
> this mortal must put on immortality. So when this
> corruptible shall have put on incorruption, and this
> mortal shall have put on immortality, then shall be
> brought to pass the saying that is written, Death is
> swallowed up in victory. O death, where is thy sting?
> O grave, where is thy victory?
>
> 1 Corinthians 15:53–55

Pastoral Prayer

Righteous and ever-living God, whose Son shattered the
power of death, bringing life and immortality to light, we
praise Thee.

Intensify our feelings that are already athrob with emotion
stirred by this death, with the joy of the resurrection that
turned night into light, sadness into laughter, and suffering
into release. Give us the peace of the resurrection that calmed
the terrorized hearts of the disciples of old. As we wait quietly
before Thee, assured of Thy power and everlastingness, speak
calm to our souls.

Until the day dawns and our home going is at hand, grant us
brave hearts, constant spirits, living to Thy praise and glory,
forever and ever, in Jesus' Spirit. Amen.

Meditation

I'LL SING, NOT CRY

Nancy Wood, a researcher of the Taos Pueblo Indians, has
written several books of poems and prose conveying their
unique philosophy. In the volume *Many Winters* she writes:

> Today is a very good day to die,
> Every living thing is in harmony with me.
> Every voice sings a chorus within me.

All beauty has come to rest in my eyes.
All bad thoughts have departed from me.
Today is a very good day to die.
My land is peaceful around me.
My fields have been turned for the last time.
My house is filled with laughter.
My children have come home,
Yes, today is a very good day to die.[1]

This conveys our feelings about the death of _____. Who would call her back to the limits of her aged body? There is an utter appropriateness about her departure, even as the author of Ecclesiastes indicates, "There is a time to be born, and a time to die (*see* Ecclesiastes 3:2).

It is appropriate because she has lived out a full, complete life [give a few details regarding her life and accomplishments].

Her death is appropriate because she was ready to die. Her house was in order and, as the poem conveys, her children have come home; everything is in harmony; all beauty has come to rest in her eyes.

It is a good time to die, because she was a Christian. She loved God, so we will sing, not cry.

Years ago one of the American churches produced a film about missionary work in Angola entitled, *I'll Sing, Not Cry*. It was based on the book *African Manhunt,* by Monroe Scott, which recounted Christ's victories in the lives of Africans. There was the story of Pastor Ngango, whose beloved wife had died. Great numbers came to the funeral, and they wailed in the customary pagan dirge of despair, until Pastor Ngango stood up by the casket and said, "Stop all this yelling and howling." The mourners stood in shocked silence. "This woman was a child of God. She has gone to her Father. I loved her, but today we are not crying, we are singing."

With that he started to sing, "Praise God," and the Christians joined him. It was not a song of despair or fear or sadness. It was a praise to God, a song of Christ's victory, a hymn of confidence.

Across the centuries comes the theme "I'll sing, not cry."

So we come to the end of a journey; it is a good day.

So today we sing, not cry! This is the end of her earthly journey, but it will continue with the dawning of a new day.

Hymn (optional)

"Beyond the Sunset"
"Abide With Me"

Benediction

O Lord, support us all the day long of our troublous life, until the shadows lengthen and the evening comes and the busy world is hushed and the fever of life is over and our work is done. Then in Thy mercy, grant us a safe lodging and a holy rest and peace at last. Amen.

Postlude

"Now the Day Is Over"

35

FOR ONE MENTALLY ILL

Prelude

"Faith," Mendelssohn
"O Rest in the Lord," Mendelssohn
"Consolation," Mendelssohn

The Opening Sentences

The Lord is nigh unto all them that call upon him, to all that call upon him in truth. He will fulfil the desire of them that fear him: he also will hear their cry, and will save them.

Psalms 145:18, 19

Invocation Prayer

Almighty God, Lord of day and night, of the stormy sea and the quiet hour, of life and death, we turn to Thee. Hear our cry. Abide with us through the storms and troubles of this mortal life so that the clouds may lift and the sea be calmed and we may see the true home of our souls, through Jesus Christ, our Lord. Amen.

Hymn (optional)

"Jesus, Savior, Pilot Me"
"Savior, Like a Shepherd Lead Us"

Old Testament Scripture Readings

General Readings:
Isaiah 40:11
Psalm 121
Deuteronomy 31:8
Deuteronomy 33:27

New Testament Scripture Readings

General Readings:
John 11:25, 26
John 14:1–3
1 Corinthians 15:35, 36, 42–44

Pastoral Prayer

Like ships storm driven into port, like starving souls that seek the bread they once despised, like wanderers begging refuge from the whelming night, like prodigals who seek the father's home when all is spent, yet welcomed at the open door, arms outstretched and kisses for our share, so is our coming to Thee, O God.

Like a still, small voice that calls us to the watches of the night, like a child's hand that feels a fast-closed door, unnoticed, and oft in vain, so is Thy coming to us, O God.

Like flowers being uplifted to the sun, like an echo to a sob-
bing cry, like a song to an aching heart, so is the assurance of
Thy peace, everlasting promise, and ever-loving presence,
through Jesus Christ. Amen.

Meditation

THE EXCITING FUTURE OF POSSIBILITY

"The best is yet to be." That assertion rings with a special
note of hope today. We have come here to honor the life of
_____ who throughout *his* years has been handicapped. He
has never been able to realize his highest potential. He has
been an inspiration in patience, courage, cooperation in the
midst of his limitation. He has been consistently cared for and
loved by parents, family, friends, and God.

Now death has set him free, coming as a cherished friend.
Death does not always appear the same. Sometimes it comes as
a dreaded enemy, intruding into a family at a most inappro-
priate time, snatching away those upon whom we depend or
who are in the prime of life. This death has come to one who
has endured slow-moving days, monotonous routine, fear, in-
security, loneliness, and who can tell what other emotional
traumas. Now he is free at last, passing from this limited life
into a new existence of amazing possibilities.

In the Scripture verse from the first Corinthian correspon-
dence, Paul gives us a glimpse of the future possibilities occa-
sioned by death. To his perplexed contemporaries he said, "It
is sown in corruption; it is raised in incorruption: It is sown in
dishonour; it is raised in glory: it is sown in weakness; it is
raised in power: It is sown a natural body; it is raised a spiritual
body. There is a natural body, and there is a spiritual body"
(1 Corinthians 15:42–44).

In these verses Paul draws four contrasts of two kinds of
bodies, which shed light on this person's future.

First, whereas the present body is corruptible, the future
body will be incorruptible. In this world everything is subject
to change and decay. "Youth's beauty fades, and manhood's

glory fades," as Sophocles, the ancient Greek poet, put it, but in the life to come there will be a permanence in which the lovely things will never cease to be lovely and beauty will never lose its sheen.

Second, whereas the present body was capable of becoming dishonored, the future body is raised in glory. In this earthly life, our bodily passions and instincts and habits can easily bring dishonor to life, but in the life to come, our bodies will no longer be servants of passion. They will be instruments for the pure service to God, for which there can be no greater honor or glory.

Third, the present body is weak; the future body will be strong. How weak is mortal man. How easily we become weary and fatigued, emotionally, mentally, and spiritually. We are limited in this life simply by exhaustion. Daily our physical condition requires food, rest, and sleep. A physical blow or a foreign element can kill the present body.

However, in the life to come, the limitations will all be gone. Here we are weak: There we will be clad with power. We will never grow weary.

Fourth, the present body is a natural body; the future body will be a spiritual body. Here we are independent vessels for the Holy Spirit, imperfect instruments of God's Spirit. In the life to come, however, the Spirit can truly fill us, use us as never possible here. In the life to come we will be able to render perfect worship, perfect service, and perfect love. "For now we see through a glass, darkly . . . but then all will be understood and known, even as we are now known" (*see* 1 Corinthians 13:12).

"If there is a physical body," and no one will deny that reality, then Paul says, "there is a spiritual body."

What an exciting existence that will be.

Walter Dudley Cavert puts the contrast in this metaphoric parable:

> In the bottom of an old pond lived some grubs who could not understand why none of their kind ever came back after crawling up the stems of the lilies to the top of the water. They promised each other that the next one who was called to make the upward

climb would return and tell what happened to him.
Soon one of them felt an urgent impulse to seek the
surface; he rested himself on the top of a lily pad and
went through a glorious transformation which made
him a dragonfly with beautiful wings. In vain he tried
to keep his promise. Flying back and forth over the
pond, he peered down at his friends below. Then he
realized that even if they could see him they would
not recognize such a radiant creature as one of their
number.[1]

The fact that we cannot see our friends or communicate with
them after the transformation, which we call death, is no proof
that they cease to exist.

Hymn (optional)

"Something Beautiful"

Benediction

But thanks be to God, which giveth us the victory
through our Lord Jesus Christ. Therefore, my beloved brethren, be ye stedfast, unmoveable, always
abounding in the work of the Lord, forasmuch as ye
know that your labour is not in vain in the Lord.

1 Corinthians 15:57, 58

36

SERVICE AT THE GRAVE

At the grave, when the people have assembled, the minister
may read one or more of the following passages.

Scripture Sentences

For I know that my Redeemer lives,
and at last he will stand upon the earth . . .
then from my flesh I shall see God,
whom I shall see on my side,
and my eyes shall behold, and not another. . . .

Job 19:25–27 RSV

. . . For I know whom I have believed, and am persuaded that he is able to keep that which I have committed unto him against that day.

2 Timothy 1:12

I have fought a good fight, I have finished my course, I have kept the faith: Henceforth there is laid up for me a crown of righteousness, which the Lord, the righteous judge, shall give me at that day: and not to me only, but unto all them also that love his appearing.

2 Timothy 4:7, 8

. . . Except a corn of wheat fall into the ground and die, it abideth alone: but if it die, it bringeth forth much fruit.

John 12:24

And I saw a new heaven and a new earth: for the first heaven and the first earth were passed away; and there was no more sea. And I John saw the holy city, new Jerusalem, coming down from God out of heaven, prepared as a bride adorned for her husband. And I heard a great voice out of heaven saying, Behold, the tabernacle of God is with men, and he will dwell with them, and they shall be his people, and God himself shall be with them, and be their God. And God shall wipe away all tears from their eyes; and there shall be no more death, neither sorrow, nor crying, neither shall there be any more pain: for the former things are pased away.

Revelation 21:1–4

FOR A CHILD

He shall feed his flock like a shepherd: he shall gather the lambs with his arm, and carry them in his bosom, and shall gently lead those that are with young.

Isaiah 40:11

Take heed that ye despise not one of these little ones; for I say unto you, That in heaven their angels do always behold the face of my Father which is in heaven.

Matthew 18:10

Let not your heart be troubled: ye believe in God, believe also in me.

John 14:1

Even so it is not the will of your Father which is in heaven, that one of these little ones should perish.

Matthew 18:14

Poems and Prose

Journey's End

We go from God *to* God—then though
    the way be long,
We shall return to Heaven our home
    at evensong.

We go from God *to* God—so let
    the space between
Be filled with beauty, conquering
    things base and mean.

We go from God *to* God—lo! What
    Transcendent bliss,
To know the journey's end will hold
    Such joy as this![1]

The tomb is not an endless night—
    It is a thoroughfare, a way

That closes in a soft twilight
And opens in eternal day.[2]

A Conquering Faith
O for a faith that will not shrink,
    Though pressed by every foe,
That will not tremble on the brink
    Of any earthly woe!

That will not murmur nor complain
    Beneath the chastening rod,
But, in the hour of grief or pain,
    Will lean upon its God.

A faith that shines more bright and clear
    When the tempests rage without,
That when in danger knows no fear,
    In darkness feels no doubt.

Lord give me such a faith as this,
    And then whate'er may come,
I'll taste e'en now the hallowed bliss
    Of an eternal home.[3]

Strong Son of God, immortal Love
    Whom we, that have not seen thy face,
    By faith, and faith alone, embrace,
Believing where we cannot prove. . . .

Thou wilt not leave us in the dust:
    Thou madest man, he knows not why,
    He thinks he was not made to die;
And thou has made him: thou art just.[4]

Footprints
One night a man dreamed he was walking along the beach
with the Lord. As scenes of his life flashed before him, he noticed that there were two sets of footprints in the sand. He also
noticed at the saddest, lowest times there was but one set of

footprints. This bothered the man. He asked the Lord, "Did you not promise that if I gave my heart to you that you would be with me all the way? Then why is there but one set of footprints during my most troublesome times?"

The Lord replied, "My precious child, I love you and would never forsake you. During those times of trial and suffering, when you see only one set of footprints, it was then I carried you."[5]

Formal Committal Services for a Christian

Cherishing memories that are forever sacred, sustained by a faith that is stronger than death, and comforted by the hope of a life that shall endless be, all that is mortal of our friend, we therefore commit to its resting place, amidst these beautiful surroundings of nature, in the assurance that if the earthly house of our tabernacle be dissolved, we have a building from God, a house not made with hands, eternal in the heavens [or, in the assurance that we have borne the image of the earthly, so shall we bear the image of the heavenly].

The reality of death has come to our circle once again. In dignity and honor, with tender affection, and solemn feelings we come to this beautiful place to depart from the physical body of our dear one. The image of that presence will linger in our minds, with joyous memories, until it will be imprinted in the glorified body for our recognition in the eons of time. Tied to faith, hope, and love—the eternal qualities—we leave here with the conviction that we do not lose our own in God's great wisdom and mercy.

Now that death has snatched from our midst _____, we come to this beautiful garden of peace, the city of the dead, to lay to rest the body of our beloved. We commend his keeping to God, whose wisdom from the beginning designed us, whose power vindicated with resurrection, our Lord Jesus Christ, and who has promised a continuing life, mysterious to us for eye has not seen, ear has not heard, and neither has it entered into the heart of man the glory that God has prepared for those who love Him. In His love, we leave the future, with trusting hope.[6]

According to the eternal plan,
    The body returns to the earth as it was,
And the spirit to God who gave it.
    Of all that is material we say,
"Earth to earth, ashes to ashes, dust to dust";
    But to the spirit we cry:
"Now thou art free,
    Free from pain and sickness and sorrow.
Free from all physical handicaps,
    Free to dream and sing and work and love.
Free to greet old friends and new
    And Jesus Christ,
And to adventure with them forever."
    Therefore we say,
"Good-bye, good-bye until tomorrow." Amen.[7]

For a Nonbeliever

A life well lived, stretching across the years, has come to its close. Under the wide spacious sky, in this garden made beautiful by trees and flowers, and amid these monuments of other dead, we lay to rest the surviving remains of our dear companion and friend. May the memory of his life ever be an inspiration until the day comes when we must take our place among these silent chambers of the dead.[8]

For a Suicide or Problem Funeral

Forasmuch as the soul of our beloved friend has passed into the life beyond, we therefore commit his body [ashes] to its resting place amidst these peaceful surroundings, relying on thy faithful word, "As a father pities his children, so the Lord pities those who fear him" (Psalms 103:13 RSV).

For a Child

In the faith of our Lord Jesus Christ, who took little children in his arms and blessed them, we commit the body [or ashes] of this dear child to his resting place amidst these beautiful [or peaceful] surroundings, in the assurance that his immortal spirit is at home with our Father in heaven.

"And they shall be mine, saith the Lord of hosts, in that day when I make up my jewels . . ." (Malachi 3:17). "They shall hunger no more, neither thirst any more; neither shall the sun light on them, nor any heat. For the Lamb which is in the midst of the throne shall feed them, and shall lead them unto living fountains of waters: and God shall wipe away all tears from their eyes." (Revelation 7:16, 17).

Now we commit to the care of our Heavenly Father this little child, trusting the compassionate, loving Savior's words, when He took children in His arms and said "of such is the kingdom of God" (Luke 18:16). "He shall feed his flock like a shepherd: he shall gather the lambs with his arm, and carry them in his bosom . . ." (Isaiah 40:11).

Inasmuch as the spirit has departed this little body, we commit his form to the earth, amidst the beautiful flowers and trees of this tranquil garden. But the true child, which is the spirit, we commend to the keeping of the Eternal Father, in whom the spirit has life everlasting, assured in the resurrection of Jesus Christ, our Lord.

The Committal Prayer
For a Child:

O tender Shepherd, carry this little lamb into the green pastures and beside the still waters of Thy paradise, among the happy company of the glorified children. Hold *him* close to Thy bosom of warmth and love so that there will be nothing to fear. When at last the mystery of Thy providence shall be unveiled to our understanding, restore this child to these yearning hearts, so that these tears of farewell may one day, as Thou hast promised, become the tears of welcome and gladness.

The Peace of God, which passes all understanding, keep your hearts and your minds in the knowledge and love of God and His Son, Jesus Christ, our Lord. Amen.

For Others:

Eternal God, from whom we come, to whom we return; we pause in the quiet of these *peaceful* [*beautiful*] surroundings to leave on the bosom of mother earth all that was mortal of our *friend* [*brother*], committing *his* spirit to Thee, *his* Creator and Redeemer, and commending into Thy loving care for comfort and guidance *his* beloved *family*.

Almighty God, our loving Father, who brought again from the dead our Lord Jesus Christ, that great Shepherd of the sheep, grant as we stand at this graveside that the voice eternal, which spoke at another sepulcher, we may hear now, saying to us, "He whom thou seekest is not here; he is risen and goeth before thee." When the sense of sorrow and loneliness weighs heavily upon us and the shadows deepen, faith falters, and hope grows dim, draw us closer to Thee, our Father; encompass us in Thy love, sustain us by Thy Spirit, and keep ever vivid the memories of our dear one, until the night is past, and with the morn may we see those angel faces smile, which we have loved long since, and lost awhile; in the name of our risen Lord, we pray. Amen.

The Benediction

Now may the God of peace who brought again from the dead our Lord Jesus, the great shepherd of the sheep, by the blood of the eternal covenant, equip you with everything good that you may do his will, working in you that which is pleasing in his sight, through Jesus Christ; to whom be glory for ever and ever. Amen.

Hebrews 13:20, 21 RSV

Unto Almighty God we commend the soul of our *brother* departed:

The Lord bless you and keep you:
The Lord make his face to shine upon you, and be gracious to you:

The Lord lift up his countenance upon you, and give you peace
in your going out and your coming in,
in your lying down and your rising up,
in your labor and in your leisure,
in your laughter and in your tears,
until you come to stand before Jesus in that day in which there
is no sunset and no dawning. Amen.[9]

O Lord, support us all the day long of this troublous life,
until the shadows lengthen and the evening comes, and the
busy world is hushed, and the fever of life is over, and our
work is done. Then of thy great mercy grant us a safe lodging,
and a holy rest, and peace at the last; through Jesus Christ our
Lord. Amen.[10]

Now the laborer's task is o'er,
Now the battle day is past,
Now, upon the farther shore
Lands the voyager at last.
　　Father in thy gracious keeping
　　Leave we now thy servant sleeping.[11]

Never forget that:
　　"after the night comes a new day,
　　after the winter another spring,
　　after the storm comes a sun-drenched earth,
　　after sin comes forgiveness,
　　after defeat comes another chance,"[12]
　　after the cross comes the resurrection,
　　after death—life.
Glory Hallelujah

SCRIPTURE APPENDIX

Selections From the Psalms

Blessed is the man that walketh not in the counsel of the ungodly, nor standeth in the way of sinners, nor sitteth in the seat of the scornful. But his delight is in the law of the Lord; and in his law doth he meditate day and night. And he shall be like a tree planted by the rivers of water, that bringeth forth his fruit in his season; his leaf also shall not wither; and whatsoever he doeth shall prosper. The ungodly are not so: but are like the chaff which the wind driveth away. Therefore the ungodly shall not stand in the judgment, nor sinners in the congregation of the righteous. For the Lord knoweth the way of the righteous: but the way of the ungodly shall perish.

Psalm 1

When I consider thy heavens, the work of thy fingers, the moon and the stars, which thou hast ordained; What is man, that thou art mindful of him? and the son of man, that thou visitest him? For thou hast made him a little lower than the angels, and hast crowned him with glory and honour. Thou madest him to have dominion over the works of thy hands; thou hast put all things under his feet: All sheep and oxen, yea, and the beasts of the field; The fowl of the air, and the fish of the sea, and whatsoever passeth through the paths of the seas.

Psalms 8:3–8

Lord, who shall abide in thy tabernacle? who shall dwell in thy holy hill? He that walketh uprightly, and worketh righteousness, and speaketh the truth in his heart. He that backbiteth not with his tongue, nor doeth evil to his neighbour, nor taketh up a reproach against his neighbour. In whose eyes a vile person is contemned; but he honoureth them that fear the Lord. He that sweareth to his own hurt, and changeth not. He that putteth not out his money to usury, nor taketh reward against the innocent. He that doeth these things shall never be moved.

Psalm 15

The Lord is my shepherd; I shall not want. He maketh me to lie down in green pastures: he leadeth me beside the still waters. He restoreth my soul: he leadeth me in the paths of righteousness for his name's sake. Yea, though I walk through the valley of the shadow of death, I will fear no evil: for thou art with me; thy rod and thy staff they comfort me. Thou preparest a table before me in the presence of mine enemies: thou anointest my head with oil; my cup runneth over. Surely goodness and mercy shall follow me all the days of my life: and I will dwell in the house of the Lord for ever.

Psalm 23

Who shall ascend into the hill of the Lord? or who shall stand in his holy place? He that hath clean hands, and a pure heart; who hath not lifted up his soul unto vanity, nor sworn deceitfully. He shall receive the blessing from the Lord, and righteousness from the God of his salvation.

Psalms 24:3–5

Unto thee, O Lord, do I lift up my soul. . . . Turn thee unto me, and have mercy upon me; for I am desolate and afflicted. The troubles of my heart are enlarged: O bring thou me out of my distresses. Look upon mine affliction and my pain; and forgive all my sins.

Psalms 25:1, 16–18

The Lord is my light and my salvation; whom shall I fear? the Lord is the strength of my life; of whom shall I be afraid? . . . Though an host should encamp against me, my heart shall not fear: though war should rise against me, in this will I be confident. One thing have I desired of the Lord, that will I seek after; that I may dwell in the house of the Lord all the days of my life, to behold the beauty of the Lord, and to enquire in his temple. For in the time of trouble he shall hide me in his pavilion: in the secret of his tabernacle shall he hide me; he shall set me up upon a rock. And now shall mine head be lifted up above mine enemies round about me: therefore will I offer in his tabernacle sacrifices of joy; I will sing, yea, I will sing praises unto the Lord. . . . I had fainted, unless I had believed to see the goodness of the Lord in the land of the living. Wait on the Lord: be of good courage, and he shall strengthen thine heart: wait, I say, on the Lord.

Psalms 27:1, 3–6, 13, 14

For his anger endureth but a moment; in his favour is life: weeping may endure for a night, but joy cometh in the morning.

Psalms 30:5

Our soul waiteth for the Lord: he is our help and our shield.

Psalms 33:20

The Lord is nigh unto them that are of a broken heart; and saveth such as be of a contrite spirit. Many are the afflictions of the righteous: but the Lord delivereth him out of them all.

Psalms 34:18, 19

Lord, make me to know mine end, and the measure of my days, what it is; that I may know how frail I am. Behold, thou hast made my days as an hand-

breadth; and mine age is as nothing before thee. . . .
And now, Lord, what wait I for? my hope is in thee.
Deliver me from all my transgressions. . . . Hear my
prayer, O Lord, and give ear unto my cry; hold not
thy peace at my tears: for I am a stranger with thee,
and a sojourner, as all my fathers were.

Psalms 39:4, 5, 7, 8, 12

As the hart panteth after the water brooks, so
panteth my soul after thee, O God. My soul thirsteth
for God, for the living God. . . . Why art thou cast
down, O my soul? and why art thou disquieted within
me? hope thou in God: for I shall yet praise him, who
is the health of my countenance, and my God.

Psalms 42:1, 2, 11

God is our refuge and strength, a very present help
in trouble. Therefore will not we fear, though the
earth be removed, and though the mountains be carried into the midst of the sea; Though the waters
thereof roar and be troubled, though the mountains
shake with the swelling thereof. There is a river, the
streams whereof shall make glad the city of God, the
holy place of the tabernacles of the most High. God is
in the midst of her; she shall not be moved: God shall
help her, and that right early.

Psalms 46:1–5

Be still, and know that I am God. . . .

Psalms 46:10

The Lord of hosts is with us; the God of Jacob is
our refuge.

Psalms 46:11

Have mercy upon me, O God, according to thy
lovingkindness: according unto the multitude of thy
tender mercies blot out my transgressions. Wash me

throughly from mine iniquity, and cleanse me from my sin. For I acknowledge my transgressions: and my sin is ever before me. Against thee, thee only, have I sinned, and done this evil in thy sight: that thou mightest be justified when thou speakest, and be clear when thou judgest. . . . Purge me with hyssop, and I shall be clean: wash me, and I shall be whiter than snow. Make me to hear joy and gladness; that the bones which thou hast broken may rejoice. Hide thy face from my sins, and blot out all mine iniquities. Create in me a clean heart, O God; and renew a right spirit within me. Cast me not away from thy presence; and take not thy holy spirit from me. Restore unto me the joy of thy salvation; and uphold me with thy free spirit.

Psalms 51:1–4, 7–12

Cast thy burden upon the Lord, and he shall sustain thee. . . .

Psalms 55:22

What time I am afraid, I will trust in thee. In God I will praise his word, in God I have put my trust; I will not fear what flesh can do unto me.

Psalms 56:3, 4

Truly my soul waiteth upon God: from him cometh my salvation. He only is my rock and my salvation. . . .

Psalms 62:1, 2

For thou art my hope, O Lord God: thou art my trust from my youth.

Psalms 71:5

Lord, thou hast been our dwelling place in all generations. Before the mountains were brought forth, or ever thou hadst formed the earth and the world, even from everlasting to everlasting, thou art God. Thou turnest man to destruction; and sayest, Return, ye children of men. For a thousand years in thy sight are but as yesterday when it is past, and as a watch in the night. Thou carriest them away as with a flood; they are as a sleep: in the morning they are like grass which groweth up. In the morning it flourisheth, and groweth up; in the evening it is cut down, and withereth. . . . The days of our years are threescore years and ten; and if by reason of strength they be fourscore years, yet is their strength labour and sorrow; for it is soon cut off, and we fly away. . . . So teach us to number our days, that we may apply our hearts unto wisdom. Return, O Lord, how long? and let it repent thee concerning thy servants. O satisfy us early with thy mercy; that we may rejoice and be glad all our days. . . . Let thy work appear unto thy servants, and thy glory unto their children. And let the beauty of the Lord our God be upon us: and establish thou the work of our hands upon us; yea, the work of our hands establish thou it.

Psalms 90:1–6, 10, 12–14, 16, 17

He that dwelleth in the secret place of the most High shall abide under the shadow of the Almighty. I will say of the Lord, He is my refuge and my fortress: my God; in him will I trust. Surely he shall deliver thee from the snare of the fowler, and from the noisome pestilence. He shall cover thee with his feathers, and under his wings shalt thou trust: his truth shall be thy shield and buckler. Thou shalt not be afraid for the terror by night; nor for the arrow that flieth by day; Nor for the pestilence that walketh in darkness; nor for the destruction that wasteth at noonday. . . . Because thou hast made the Lord, which is my refuge, even the most High, thy habitation; There shall no evil befall thee, neither shall any plague come nigh thy dwelling.

Psalms 91:1–6, 9, 10

Bless the Lord, O my soul: and all that is within me, bless his holy name. Bless the Lord, O my soul, and forget not all his benefits. . . .

Psalms 103:1, 2

Bless the Lord, O my soul, and forget not all his benefits: Who forgiveth all thine iniquities; who healeth all thy diseases; Who redeemeth thy life from destruction; who crowneth thee with lovingkindness and tender mercies. . . .

Psalms 103:2–4

For as the heaven is high above the earth, so great is his mercy toward them that fear him. . . . Like as a father pitieth his children, so the Lord pitieth them that fear him. For he knoweth our frame; he remembereth that we are dust. As for man, his days are as grass: as a flower of the field, so he flourisheth. For the wind passeth over it, and it is gone; and the place thereof shall know it no more. But the mercy of the Lord is from everlasting to everlasting upon them that fear him, and his righteousness unto children's children; To such as keep his covenant, and to those that remember his commandments to do them.

Psalms 103:11, 13–18

I love the Lord, because he hath heard my voice and my supplications. Because he hath inclined his ear unto me, therefore will I call upon him as long as I live. The sorrows of death compassed me, and the pains of hell gat hold upon me: I found trouble and sorrow. Then called I upon the name of the Lord; O Lord, I beseech thee, deliver my soul. Gracious is the Lord, and righteous; yea, our God is merciful. The Lord preserveth the simple: I was brought low, and he helped me. Return unto thy rest, O my soul; for the Lord hath dealt bountifully with thee. For thou hast delivered my soul from death, mine eyes from tears, and my feet from falling. . . . I believed, therefore have I spoken: I was greatly afflicted. . . . What shall I render unto the Lord for all his benefits toward me? I will take the cup of salvation, and call upon the name of the Lord. I will pay my vows unto the Lord now in the presence of all his people. Precious in the sight of the Lord is the death of his saints.

Psalms 116:1–8, 10, 12–15

Wherewithal shall a young man cleanse his way? by taking heed thereto according to thy word. With my whole heart have I sought thee: O let me not wander from thy commandments. Thy word have I hid in mine heart, that I might not sin against thee. Blessed art thou, O Lord: teach me thy statutes. With my lips have I declared all the judgments of thy mouth. I have rejoiced in the way of thy testimonies, as much as in all riches. I will meditate in thy precepts, and have respect unto thy ways. I will delight myself in thy statutes: I will not forget thy word.

Psalms 119:9–16

Before I was afflicted I went astray: but now have I kept thy word. . . . It is good for me that I have been afflicted; that I might learn thy statutes.

Psalms 119:67, 71

Look thou upon me, and be merciful unto me, as thou usest to do unto those that love thy name. Order my steps in thy word: and let not any iniquity have dominion over me. Deliver me from the oppression of man: so will I keep thy precepts. Make thy face to shine upon thy servant; and teach me thy statutes. Rivers of waters run down mine eyes, because they keep not thy law.

Psalms 119:132–136

I will lift up mine eyes unto the hills, from whence cometh my help. My help cometh from the Lord, which made heaven and earth. He will not suffer thy foot to be moved: he that keepeth thee will not slumber. Behold, he that keepeth Israel shall neither slumber nor sleep. The Lord is thy keeper: the Lord is thy shade upon thy right hand. The sun shall not smite thee by day, nor the moon by night. The Lord shall preserve thee from all evil: he shall preserve thy soul. The Lord shall preserve thy going out and thy coming in from this time forth, and even for evermore.

Psalm 121

Our help is in the name of the Lord, who made heaven and earth.

Psalms 124:8

Out of the depths have I cried unto thee, O Lord. Lord, hear my voice: let thine ears be attentive to the voice of my supplications. If thou, Lord, shouldest mark iniquities, O Lord, who shall stand? But there is forgiveness with thee, that thou mayest be feared. I wait for the Lord, my soul doth wait, and in his word do I hope. My soul waiteth for the Lord more than they that watch for the morning: I say, more than they that watch for the morning. Let Israel hope in the Lord: for with the Lord there is mercy, and with him is plenteous redemption. And he shall redeem Israel from all his iniquities.

Psalm 130

O Lord, thou hast searched me, and known me. Thou knowest my downsitting and mine uprising, thou understandest my thought afar off. Thou compassest my path and my lying down, and art acquainted with all my ways. For there is not a word in my tongue, but, lo, O Lord, thou knowest it altogether. Thou has beset me behind and before, and laid thine hand upon me. Such knowledge is too wonderful for me; it is high, I cannot attain unto it. Whither shall I go from thy spirit? or whither shall I flee from thy presence? If I ascend up into heaven, thou art there: if I make my bed in hell, behold, thou art there. If I take the wings of the morning, and dwell in the uttermost parts of the sea; Even there shall thy hand lead me, and thy right hand shall hold me. If I say, Surely the darkness shall cover me; even the night shall be light about me. Yea, the darkness hideth not from thee; but the night shineth as the day: the darkness and the light are both alike to thee. . . . How precious also are thy thoughts unto me, O God! how great is the sum of them! If I should count them, they are more in number than the sand: when I awake, I am still with thee.

Psalms 139:1–12, 17, 18

Search me, O God, and know my heart: try me, and know my thoughts: And see if there be any wicked way in me, and lead me in the way everlasting.

Psalms 139:23, 24

The Lord is nigh unto all them that call upon him, to all that call upon him in truth.

Psalms 145:18

Praise ye the Lord: for it is good to sing praises unto our God; for it is pleasant; and praise is comely. The Lord doth build up Jerusalem: he gathereth together the outcasts of Israel. He healeth the broken in heart, and bindeth up their wounds.

Psalms 147:1–3

Selections From the Old Testament

In the beginning God created the heaven and the earth. And the earth was without form, and void; and darkness was upon the face of the deep. And the Spirit of God moved upon the face of the waters. And God said, Let there be light: and there was light. And God saw the light, that it was good: and God divided the light from the darkness. And God called the light Day, and the darkness he called Night. And the evening and the morning were the first day. . . . And God said, Let the earth bring forth the living creature after his kind . . . and cattle after their kind, and every thing that creepeth upon the earth after his kind: and God saw that it was good. And God said, Let us make man in our image, after our likeness: and let them have dominion over the fish of the sea, and over the fowl of the air, and over the cattle, and over all the earth, and over every creeping thing that creepeth upon the earth. So God created man in his own image, in the image of God created he him; male and female created he them. And God blessed them, and God said unto them, Be fruitful, and multiply, and replenish the earth, and subdue it: and have dominion over the fish of the sea, and over the fowl of the air, and over every living thing that moveth upon the earth. . . . And God saw every thing that he had made, and, behold, it was very good. And the evening and the morning were the sixth day.

Genesis 1:1–5, 24–28, 31

Now these are the commandments, the statutes, and the judgments, which the Lord your God commanded to teach you, that ye might do them in the land whither ye go to possess it: That thou mightest fear the Lord thy God, to keep all his statutes and his commandments, which I command thee, thou, and thy son, and thy son's son, all the days of thy life; and that thy days may be prolonged. Hear therefore, O Israel, and observe to do it; that it may be well with thee, and that ye may increase mightily, as the Lord God of thy fathers hath promised thee, in the land that floweth with milk and honey. Hear, O Israel: The Lord our God is one Lord: And thou shalt love the Lord thy God with all thine heart, and with all thy soul, and with all thy might. And these words, which I command thee this day, shall be in thine heart: And thou shalt teach them diligently unto thy children, and shalt talk of them when thou sittest in thine house, and when thou walkest by the way, and when thou liest down, and when thou risest up. And thou shalt bind them for a sign upon thine hand, and they shall be as frontlets between thine eyes. And thou shalt write them upon the posts of thy house, and on thy gates.

Deuteronomy 6:1–9

But if from thence thou shalt seek the Lord thy God, thou shalt find him, if thou seek him with all thy heart and with all thy soul. When thou art in tribulation, and all these things are come upon thee, even in the latter days, if thou turn to the Lord thy God, and shalt be obedient unto his voice; (For the Lord thy God is a merciful God;) he will not forsake thee; neither destroy thee, nor forget the covenant of thy fathers which he sware unto them.

Deuteronomy 4:29–31

And the Lord, he it is that doth go before thee; he will be with thee, he will not fail thee, neither forsake thee: fear not, neither be dismayed.

Deuteronomy 31:8

The eternal God is thy refuge, and underneath are the everlasting arms. . . .

Deuteronomy 33:27

Now after the death of Moses the servant of the Lord it came to pass, that the Lord spake unto Joshua the son of Nun, Moses' minister, saying, Moses my servant is dead; now therefore arise, go over this Jordan, thou, and all this people, unto the land which I do give to them, even to the children of Israel. . . . There shall not any man be able to stand before thee all the days of thy life: as I was with Moses, so I will be with thee: I will not fail thee, nor forsake thee. . . .

Only be thou strong and very courageous, that thou mayest observe to do according to all the law, which Moses my servant commanded thee: turn not from it to the right hand or to the left, that thou mayest prosper whithersoever thou goest. . . . Have not I commanded thee? Be strong and of a good courage; be not afraid, neither be thou dismayed: for the Lord thy God is with thee whithersoever thou goest.

Joshua 1:1, 2, 5, 7, 9

. . . Be strong and of a good courage; be not afraid, neither be thou dismayed: for the Lord thy God is with thee whithersoever thou goest.

Joshua 1:9

And Nathan departed unto his house. And the Lord struck the child that Uriah's wife bare unto David, and it was very sick. David therefore besought God for the child; and David fasted, and went in, and lay all night upon the earth. And the elders of his house arose, and went to him, to raise him up from the earth: but he would not, neither did he eat bread with them. And it came to pass on the seventh day, that the child died. And the servants of David feared to tell him that the child was dead: for they said, Behold, while the child was yet alive, we spake unto him, and he would not hearken unto our voice: how will he then vex himself, if we tell him that the child is dead? But when David saw that his servants whispered, David perceived that the child was dead: therefore David said unto his servants, Is the child dead? And they said, He is dead. Then David arose from the earth, and washed, and anointed himself, and changed his apparel, and came into the house of the Lord, and worshipped: then he came to his own house; and when he required, they set bread before him, and he did eat. Then said his servants unto him, What thing is this that thou hast done? thou didst fast and weep for the child, while it was alive; but when

the child was dead, thou didst rise and eat bread. And
he said, While the child was yet alive, I fasted and
wept: for I said, Who can tell whether God will be
gracious to me, that the child may live? But now he is
dead, wherefore should I fast? can I bring him back
again? I shall go to him, but he shall not return to me.

2 Samuel 12:15–23

And he said, The Lord is my rock, and my fortress,
and my deliverer; The God of my rock; in him will I
trust: he is my shield, and the horn of my salvation,
my high tower, and my refuge, my saviour; thou
savest me from violence.

2 Samuel 22:2, 3

Then she saddled an ass, and said to her servant,
Drive, and go forward; slack not thy riding for me,
except I bid thee. So she went and came unto the man
of God to mount Carmel. And it came to pass, when
the man of God saw her afar off, that he said to Gehazi his servant, Behold, yonder is that Shunammite:
Run now, I pray thee, to meet her, and say unto her,
Is it well with thee? is it well with thy husband? is
it well with the child? And she answered, It is well.

2 Kings 4:24–26

Behold, happy is the man whom God correcteth:
therefore despise not thou the chastening of the Almighty: For he maketh sore, and bindeth up: he
woundeth, and his hands make whole. . . . And thou
shalt know that thy tabernacle shall be in peace; and
thou shalt visit thy habitation, and shalt not sin. Thou
shalt know also that thy seed shall be great, and thine
offspring as the grass of the earth. Thou shalt come to
thy grave in a full age, like as a shock of corn cometh
in in his season. Lo this, we have searched it, so it is,
hear it, and know thou it for thy good.

Job 5:17, 18, 24–27

Oh that my words were now written! oh that they were printed in a book! That they were graven with an iron pen and lead in the rock for ever! For I know that my redeemer liveth, and that he shall stand at the latter day upon the earth: And though after my skin worms destroy this body, yet in my flesh shall I see God: Whom I shall see for myself, and mine eyes shall behold, and not another. . . .

Job 19:23–27

Who can find a virtuous woman? for her price is far above rubies. The heart of her husband doth safely trust in her, so that he shall have no need of spoil. She will do him good and not evil all the days of her life. . . . She stretcheth out her hand to the poor; yea, she reacheth forth her hands to the needy. . . . Strength and honour are her clothing; and she shall rejoice in time to come. She openeth her mouth with wisdom; and in her tongue is the law of kindness. She looketh well to the ways of her household, and eateth not the bread of idleness. Her children arise up, and call her blessed; her husband also, and he praiseth her. Many daughters have done virtuously, but thou excellest them all. Favour is deceitful, and beauty is vain: but a woman that feareth the Lord, she shall be praised. Give her of the fruit of her hands; and let her own works praise her in the gates.

Proverbs 31:10–12, 20, 25–31

[There is] a time to be born and a time to die;
a time to plant and a time to uproot . . .
a time to weep and a time to laugh;
a time for mourning and a time for dancing . . .
a time to seek and a time to lose;
a time to keep and a time to throw away . . .
a time for silence and a time for speech;
a time to love . . . a time for peace.

Ecclesiastes 3:2, 4, 6–8 NEB

I have seen the business that God has given to the
sons of men to be busy with. He has made everything
beautiful in its time; also he has put eternity into
man's mind. . . .

Ecclesiastes 3:10, 11 RSV

Thou wilt keep him in perfect peace, whose mind is
stayed on thee: because he trusteth in thee.

Isaiah 26:3

Strengthen ye the weak hands, and confirm the
feeble knees. Say to them that are of a fearful heart,
Be strong, fear not: behold, your God will come with
vengeance, even God with a recompence; he will
come and save you. Then the eyes of the blind shall
be opened, and the ears of the deaf shall be unstopped. Then shall the lame man leap as an hart,
and the tongue of the dumb sing: for in the wilderness
shall waters break out, and streams in the desert. And
the parched ground shall become a pool, and the
thirsty land springs of water: in the habitation of
dragons, where each lay, shall be grass with reeds and
rushes. And an highway shall be there, and a way,
and it shall be called The way of holiness; the unclean
shall not pass over it; but it shall be for those: the
wayfaring men, though fools, shall not err therein.
No lion shall be there, nor any ravenous beast shall
go up thereon, it shall not be found there; but the redeemed shall walk there: And the ransomed of the
Lord shall return, and come to Zion with songs and
everlasting joy upon their heads: they shall obtain joy
and gladness, and sorrow and sighing shall flee away.

Isaiah 35:3–10

Comfort ye, comfort ye my people, saith your God.
. . . Thou art my servant; I have chosen thee, and not
cast thee away. Fear thou not; for I am with thee: be
not dismayed; for I am thy God: I will strengthen

thee; yea, I will help thee; yea, I will uphold thee with the right hand of my righteousness. . . . For I the Lord thy God will hold thy right hand, saying unto thee, Fear not; I will help thee.

Isaiah 40:1; 41:9, 10, 13

He shall feed his flock like a shepherd: he shall gather the lambs with his arm, and carry them in his bosom. . . .

Isaiah 40:11

But they that wait upon the Lord shall renew their strength; they shall mount up with wings as eagles; they shall run, and not be weary; and they shall walk, and not faint.

Isaiah 40:31

Fear thou not; for I am with thee: be not dismayed; for I am thy God: I will strengthen thee; yea, I will help thee; yea, I will uphold thee with the right hand of my righteousness. . . . For I the Lord thy God will hold thy right hand, saying unto thee, Fear not; I will help thee.

Isaiah 41:10, 13

. . . Fear not: for I have redeemed thee, I have called thee by thy name; thou art mine. When thou passest through the waters, I will be with thee; and through the rivers, they shall not overflow thee: when thou walkest through the fire, thou shalt not be burned; neither shall the flame kindle upon thee. For I am the Lord thy God, the Holy One of Israel, thy Saviour. . . .

Isaiah 43:1–3

. . . but with everlasting kindness will I have mercy on thee, saith the Lord thy Redeemer. . . . For the mountains shall depart, and the hills be removed; but my kindness shall not depart from thee, neither shall the covenant of my peace be removed, saith the Lord that hath mercy on thee.

Isaiah 54:8, 10

Seek ye the Lord while he may be found, call ye upon him while he is near.

Isaiah 55:6

Arise, shine; for thy light is come, and the glory of the Lord is risen upon thee. For, behold, the darkness shall cover the earth, and gross darkness the people: but the Lord shall arise upon thee, and his glory shall be seen upon thee. And the Gentiles shall come to thy light, and kings to the brightness of thy rising. . . . The sun shall be no more thy light by day; neither for brightness shall the moon give light unto thee: but the Lord shall be unto thee an everlasting light, and thy God thy glory. Thy sun shall no more go down; neither shall thy moon withdraw itself: for the Lord shall be thine everlasting light, and the days of thy mourning shall be ended.

Isaiah 60:1–3, 19, 20

Thus saith the Lord; A voice was heard in Ramah, lamentation, and bitter weeping; Rahel weeping for her children refused to be comforted for her children, because they were not. Thus saith the Lord; Refrain thy voice from weeping, and thine eyes from tears: for thy work shall be rewarded, saith the Lord. . . .

Jeremiah 31:15, 16

. . . But the Lord will be the hope of his people, and the strength of the children of Israel.

Joel 3:16

The Lord is good, a strong hold in the day of trouble; and he knoweth them that trust in him.

Nahum 1:7

And the streets of the city shall be full of boys and girls playing in the streets thereof.

Zechariah 8:5

Selections From the New Testament

Blessed are the poor in spirit: for their's is the kingdom of heaven. Blessed are they that mourn: for they shall be comforted. Blessed are the meek: for they shall inherit the earth. Blessed are they which do hunger and thirst after righteousness: for they shall be filled. Blessed are the merciful: for they shall obtain mercy. Blessed are the pure in heart: for they shall see God. Blessed are the peacemakers: for they shall be called the children of God. Blessed are they which are persecuted for righteousness' sake: for their's is the kingdom of heaven. Blessed are ye, when men shall revile you, and persecute you, and shall say all manner of evil against you falsely, for my sake. Rejoice, and be exceeding glad: for great is your reward in heaven: for so persecuted they the prophets which were before you. Ye are the salt of the earth: but if the salt have lost his savour, wherewith shall it be salted? it is thenceforth good for nothing, but to be cast out, and to be trodden under foot of men. Ye are the light of the world. A city that is set on an hill cannot be hid. Neither do men light a candle, and put it under a bushel, but on a candlestick; and it giveth light unto all that are in the house. Let your light so shine before men, that they may see your good works, and glorify your Father which is in heaven.

Matthew 5:3–16

Lay not up for yourselves treasures upon earth, where moth and rust doth corrupt, and where thieves break through and steal: But lay up for yourselves treasures in heaven, where neither moth nor rust doth corrupt, and where thieves do not break through nor steal: For where your treasure is, there will your heart be also. . . . But seek ye first the kingdom of God, and his righteousness; and all these things shall be added unto you.

Matthew 6:19–21, 33

Therefore whosoever heareth these sayings of mine, and doeth them, I will liken him unto a wise man, which built his house upon a rock: And the rain descended, and the floods came, and the winds blew, and beat upon that house; and it fell not: for it was founded upon a rock. And every one that heareth these sayings of mine, and doeth them not, shall be likened unto a foolish man, which built his house upon the sand: And the rain descended, and the floods came, and the winds blew, and beat upon that house; and it fell: and great was the fall of it.

Matthew 7:24–27

Come unto me, all ye that labour and are heavy laden, and I will give you rest. Take my yoke upon you, and learn of me; for I am meek and lowly in heart: and ye shall find rest unto your souls. For my yoke is easy, and my burden is light.

Matthew 11:28–30

At the same time came the disciples unto Jesus, saying, Who is the greatest in the kingdom of heaven? And Jesus called a little child unto him, and set him in the midst of them, And said, Verily I say unto you, Except ye be converted, and become as little children, ye shall not enter into the kingdom of heaven. Whosoever therefore shall humble himself as this little child, the same is greatest in the kingdom of heaven. And whoso shall receive one such little child in my name receiveth me. . . . Take heed that ye despise not one of these little ones; for I say unto you, That in heaven their angels do always behold the face of my Father which is in heaven. . . . And they brought young children to him, that he should touch them: and his disciples rebuked those that brought them. But when Jesus saw it, he was much displeased, and said unto them, Suffer the little children to come unto me, and forbid them not: for of such is the kingdom of God. Verily I say unto you, Whosoever shall not receive the kingdom of God as a little child, he shall not enter therein. And he took them up in his arms, put his hands upon them, and blessed them.

Matthew 18:1–5, 10; Mark 10:13–16

While he yet spake, there came from the ruler of the synagogue's house certain which said, Thy daughter is dead: why troublest thou the Master any further? As soon as Jesus heard the word that was spoken, he saith unto the ruler of the synagogue, Be not afraid, only believe. And he suffered no man to follow him, save Peter, and James, and John the brother of James. And he cometh to the house of the ruler of the synagogue, and seeth the tumult, and them that wept and wailed greatly. And when he was come in, he saith unto them, Why make ye this ado, and weep? the damsel is not dead, but sleepeth. And they laughed him to scorn. But when he had put them all out, he taketh the father and the mother of the damsel, and them that were with him, and entereth in where the damsel was lying. And he took the damsel by the hand, and said unto her, Talithacumi; which is, being interpreted, Damsel, I say unto thee, arise. And straightway the damsel arose, and walked; for she was of the age of twelve years. And they were astonished with a great astonishment. And he charged them straitly that no man should know it; and commanded that something should be given her to eat.

Mark 5:35–43

And it came to pass the day after, that he went into a city called Nain; and many of his disciples went with him, and much people. Now when he came nigh to the gate of the city, behold, there was a dead man carried out, the only son of his mother, and she was a widow: and much people of the city was with her. And when the Lord saw her, he had compassion on her, and said unto her, Weep not. And he came and touched the bier: and they that bare him stood still. And he said, Young man, I say unto thee, Arise. And he that was dead sat up, and began to speak. And he delivered him to his mother.

Luke 7:11–15

Are not five sparrows sold for two farthings, and not one of them is forgotten before God? But even the very hairs of your head are all numbered. Fear not therefore: ye are of more value than many sparrows.

Luke 12:6, 7

For as the Father raiseth up the dead, and quickeneth them; even so the Son quickeneth whom he will. For the Father judgeth no man, but hath committed all judgment unto the Son: That all men should honour the Son, even as they honour the Father. He that honoureth not the Son honoureth not the Father which hath sent him. Verily, verily, I say unto you, He that heareth my word, and believeth on him that sent me, hath everlasting life, and shall not come into condemnation; but is passed from death unto life. Verily, verily, I say unto you, The hour is coming, and now is, when the dead shall hear the voice of the Son of God: and they that hear shall live. For as the Father hath life in himself; so hath he given to the Son to have life in himself; And hath given him authority to execute judgment also, because he is the Son of man. Marvel not at this: for the hour is coming, in the which all that are in the graves shall hear his voice, And shall come forth; they that have done good, unto the resurrection of life; and they that have done evil, unto the resurrection of damnation.

John 5:21–29

Jesus said unto her, I am the resurrection, and the life: he that believeth in me, though he were dead, yet shall he live: And whosoever liveth and believeth in me shall never die. Believest thou this?

John 11:25, 26

Let not your heart be troubled: ye believe in God, believe also in me. In my Father's house are many mansions: if it were not so, I would have told you. I go to prepare a place for you. And if I go and prepare a place for you, I will come again, and receive you unto myself; that where I am, there ye may be also.

John 14:1–3

I will not leave you comfortless: I will come to you. . . . Peace I leave with you, my peace I give unto you: not as the world giveth, give I unto you. Let not your heart be troubled, neither let it be afraid.

John 14:18, 27

If ye love me, keep my commandments. And I will pray the Father, and he shall give you another Comforter, that he may abide with you for ever; Even the Spirit of truth; whom the world cannot receive, because it seeth him not, neither knoweth him: but ye know him; for he dwelleth with you, and shall be in you. . . . Peace I leave with you, my peace I give unto you: not as the world giveth, give I unto you. Let not your heart be troubled, neither let it be afraid.

John 14:15–17, 27

. . . In the world ye shall have tribulation: but be of good cheer; I have overcome the world.

John 16:33

For as many as are led by the Spirit of God, they are the sons of God. . . . The Spirit itself beareth witness with our spirit, that we are the children of God: And if children, then heirs; heirs of God, and joint-heirs with Christ; if so be that we suffer with him, that we may be also glorified together. For I reckon that the sufferings of this present time are not worthy to be compared with the glory which shall be revealed in us.... If God be for us, who can be against us? He that spared not his own Son, but delivered him up for us all, how shall he not with him also freely give us all things? Who shall lay any thing to the charge of God's elect? It is God that justifieth. Who is he that condemneth? It is Christ that died, yea rather, that is risen again, who is even at the right hand of God, who also maketh intercession for us.

Romans 8:14, 16–18, 31–34

And we know that all things work together for good to them that love God....

Romans 8:28

Who shall separate us from the love of Christ? shall tribulation, or distress, or persecution, or famine, or nakedness, or peril, or sword?... Nay, in all these things we are more than conquerors through him that loved us. For I am persuaded, that neither death, nor life, nor angels, nor principalities, nor powers, nor things present, nor things to come, Nor height, nor depth, nor any other creature, shall be able to separate us from the love of God, which is in Christ Jesus our Lord.

Romans 8:35, 37–39

For whether we live, we live unto the Lord; and whether we die, we die unto the Lord: whether we live therefore, or die, we are the Lord's. For to this end Christ both died, and rose, and revived, that he might be Lord both of the dead and living.

Romans 14:8, 9

Beloved, now are we children of God, and it is not yet made manifest what we shall be. We know that, if he shall be manifested, we shall be like him; for we shall see him even as he is. . . . now we see in a mirror, darkly; but then face to face: now I know in part; but then shall I know fully even as also I was fully known.

1 John 3:2; 1 Corinthians 13:12 ASV

Now if Christ be preached that he rose from the dead, how say some among you that there is no resurrection of the dead? . . . And if Christ be not raised, your faith is vain; ye are yet in your sins. . . . If in this life only we have hope in Christ, we are of all men most miserable. But now is Christ risen from the dead, and become the firstfruits of them that slept. For since by man came death, by man came also the resurrection of the dead. For as in Adam all die, even so in Christ shall all be made alive.

1 Corinthians 15:12, 17, 19–22

But some man will say, How are the dead raised up? and with what body do they come? Thou fool, that which thou sowest is not quickened, except it die. . . . So also is the resurrection of the dead. It is sown in corruption; it is raised in incoruption: It is sown in dishonour; it is raised in glory: it is sown in weakness; it is raised in power: It is sown a natural body; it is raised a spiritual body. There is a natural body, and there is a spiritual body.

1 Corinthians 15:35, 36, 42–44

For this corruptible must put on incorruption, and this mortal must put on immortality. So when this corruptible shall have put on incorruption, and this mortal shall have put on immortality, then shall be brought to pass the saying that is written, Death is swallowed up in victory. O death, where is thy sting? O grave, where is thy victory? The sting of death is sin; and the strength of sin is the law. But thanks be to God, which giveth us the victory through our Lord

Jesus Christ. Therefore, my beloved brethren, be ye stedfast, unmoveable, always abounding in the work of the Lord, forasmuch as ye know that your labour is not in vain in the Lord.

1 Corinthians 15:53–58

Blessed be God, even the Father of our Lord Jesus Christ, the Father of mercies, and the God of all comfort; Who comforteth us in all our tribulation, that we may be able to comfort them which are in any trouble, by the comfort wherewith we ourselves are comforted of God.

2 Corinthians 1:3, 4

For which cause we faint not; but though our outward man perish, yet the inward man is renewed day by day. For our light affliction, which is but for a moment, worketh for us a far more exceeding and eternal weight of glory; While we look not at the things which are seen, but at the things which are not seen: for the things which are seen are temporal; but the things which are not seen are eternal.

2 Corinthians 4:16–18

For we know that if our earthly house of this tabernacle were dissolved, we have a building of God, an house not made with hands, eternal in the heavens. For in this we groan, earnestly desiring to be clothed upon with our house which is from heaven: If so be that being clothed we shall not be found naked. For we that are in this tabernacle do groan, being burdened: not for that we would be unclothed, but clothed upon, that mortality might be swallowed up of life. Now he that hath wrought us for the selfsame thing is God, who also hath given unto us the earnest of the Spirit. Therefore we are always confident, knowing that, whilst we are at home in the body, we are absent from the Lord: (For we walk by faith, not by sight:) We are confident, I say, and willing rather to be absent from the body, and to be present with the Lord. Wherefore we labour, that, whether present or absent, we may be accepted of him.

2 Corinthians 5:1–9

... My grace is sufficient for thee: for my strength is made perfect in weakness. ...

2 Corinthians 12:9

For this cause I bow my knees unto the Father of our Lord Jesus Christ, Of whom the whole family in heaven and earth is named, That he would grant you, according to the riches of his glory, to be strengthened with might by his Spirit in the inner man; That Christ may dwell in your hearts by faith; that ye, being rooted and grounded in love, May be able to comprehend with all saints what is the breadth, and length, depth, and height; And to know the love of Christ, which passeth knowledge, that ye might be filled with all the fulness of God. Now unto him that is able to do exceeding abundantly above all that we ask or think, according to the power that worketh in us, Unto him be glory in the church by Christ Jesus throughout all ages, world without end. Amen.

Ephesians 3:14–21

But what things were gain to me, those I counted loss for Christ. Yea doubtless, and I count all things but loss for the excellency of the knowledge of Christ Jesus my Lord: for whom I have suffered the loss of all things, and do count them but dung, that I may win Christ, And be found in him, not having mine own righteousness, which is of the law, but that which is through the faith of Christ, the righteousness which is of God by faith: That I may know him, and the power of his resurrection, and the fellowship of his sufferings, being made conformable unto his death; If by any means I might attain unto the resurrection of the dead. Not as though I had already attained, either were already perfect: but I follow after, if that I may apprehend that for which also I am apprehended of Christ Jesus. Brethren, I count not myself to have apprehended: but this one thing I do, forgetting those things which are behind, and reaching forth unto those things which are before, I press toward the mark for the prize of the high calling of God in Christ Jesus. Let us therefore, as many as be perfect, be thus minded: and if any thing ye be otherwise minded, God shall reveal even this unto you. Nevertheless, whereto we have already attained. . . .

Philippians 3:7–16

But I would not have you to be ignorant, brethren, concerning them which are asleep, that ye sorrow not, even as others which have no hope. For if we believe that Jesus died and rose again, even so them also which sleep in Jesus will God bring with him.

1 Thessalonians 4:13, 14

But is now made manifest by the appearing of our Saviour Jesus Christ, who hath abolished death, and hath brought life and immortality to light through the gospel.

2 Timothy 1:10

For I am now ready to be offered, and the time of my departure is at hand. I have fought a good fight, I have finished my course, I have kept the faith: Henceforth there is laid up for me a crown of righteousness, which the Lord, the righteous judge, shall give me at that day: and not to me only, but unto all them also that love his appearing.

2 Timothy 4:6–8

For the grace of God that bringeth salvation hath appeared to all men, Teaching us that, denying ungodliness and worldly lusts, we should live soberly, righteously, and godly, in this present world; Looking for that blessed hope, and the glorious appearing of the great God and our Saviour Jesus Christ; Who gave himself for us, that he might redeem us from all iniquity, and purify unto himself a peculiar people, zealous of good works.

Titus 2:11–14

Let us therefore come boldly unto the throne of grace, that we may obtain mercy, and find grace to help in time of need.

Hebrews 4:16

Wherefore seeing we also are compassed about with so great a cloud of witnessses, let us lay aside every weight, and the sin which doth so easily beset us, and let us run with patience the race that is set before us, Looking unto Jesus the author and finisher of our faith; who for the joy that was set before him endured the cross, despising the shame, and is set down at the right hand of the throne of God.

Hebrews 12:1, 2

Blessed be the God and Father of our Lord Jesus Christ, which according to his abundant mercy hath begotten us again unto a lively hope by the resurrection of Jesus Christ from the dead, To an inheritance incorruptible, and undefiled, and that fadeth not away, reserved in heaven for you, Who are kept by the power of God through faith unto salvation ready to be revealed in the last time. Wherein ye greatly rejoice, though now for a season, if need be, ye are in heaviness through manifold temptations: That the trial of your faith being much more precious than of gold that perisheth, though it be tried with fire, might be found unto praise and honour and glory at the appearing of Jesus Christ: Whom having not seen, ye love; in whom, though now ye see him not, yet believing, ye rejoice with joy unspeakable and full of glory: Receiving the end of your faith, even the salvation of your souls.

1 Peter 1:3–9

But, beloved, be not ignorant of this one thing, that one day is with the Lord as a thousand years, and a thousand years as one day. The Lord is not slack concerning his promise, as some men count slackness; but is longsuffering to us-ward, not willing that any should perish, but that all should come to repentance. But the day of the Lord will come as a thief in the night; in the which the heavens shall pass away with a great noise, and the elements shall melt with fervent heat, the earth also and the works that are therein shall be burned up. Seeing then that all these things shall be dissolved, what manner of persons ought ye to be in all holy conversation and godliness, Looking for and hasting unto the coming of the day of God, wherein the heavens being on fire shall be dissolved, and the elements shall melt with fervent heat? Nevertheless we, according to his promise, look for new heavens and a new earth, wherein dwelleth righteousness. Wherefore, beloved, seeing that ye look for such things, be diligent that ye may be found of him in peace, without spot, and blameless.

2 Peter 3:8–14

Beloved, think it not strange concerning the fiery trial which is to try you, as though some strange thing happened unto you: But rejoice, inasmuch as ye are partakers of Christ's sufferings; that, when his glory shall be revealed, ye may be glad also with exceeding joy.

1 Peter 4:12, 13

Beloved, let us love one another: for love is of God; and every one that loveth is born of God, and knoweth God. He that loveth not knoweth not God;

for God is love. In this was manifested the love of God toward us, because that God sent his only begotten Son into the world, that we might live through him. Herein is love, not that we loved God, but that he loved us, and sent his Son to be the propitiation for our sins. Beloved, if God so loved us, we ought also to love one another. No man hath seen God at any time. If we love one another, God dwelleth in us, and his love is perfected in us.

1 John 4:7–12

... God is love; and he that dwelleth in love dwelleth in God, and God in him. Herein is our love made perfect, that we may have boldness in the day of judgment: because as he is, so are we in this world. There is no fear in love; but perfect love casteth out fear: because fear hath torment. He that feareth is not made perfect in love. We love him, because he first loved us. If a man say, I love God, and hateth his brother, he is a liar: for he that loveth not his brother whom he hath seen, how can he love God whom he hath not seen? And this commandment have we from him, That he who loveth God love his brother also.

1 John 4:16–21

After this I beheld, and, lo, a great multitude, which no man could number, of all nations, and kindreds, and people, and tongues, stood before the throne, and before the Lamb, clothed with white robes, and palms in their hands; And cried with a loud voice, saying, Salvation to our God which sitteth upon the throne, and unto the Lamb. And all the angels stood round about the throne, and about the elders and the four beasts, and fell before the throne on their faces, and worshipped God, Saying, Amen: Blessing, and glory, and wisdom, and thanksgiving, and honour, and power, and might, be unto our God for ever and ever. Amen. And one of the elders answered, saying unto me, What are these which are arrayed in white robes? and whence came they? And I said unto him, Sir, thou knowest. And he said to me, These are they which came out of great tribulation, and have washed their robes, and made them white in the blood of the Lamb. Therefore are they before the throne of God, and serve him day and night in his temple: and he that sitteth on the throne shall dwell among them. They shall hunger no more, neither thirst any more; neither shall the sun light on them, nor any heat. For the Lamb which is in the midst of the throne shall feed them, and shall lead them unto living fountains of waters: and God shall wipe away all tears from their eyes.

Revelation 7:9–17

They shall hunger no more, neither thirst any more; neither shall the sun light on them, nor any heat. For the Lamb which is in the midst of the throne shall feed them, and shall lead them unto living fountains of waters: and God shall wipe away all tears from their eyes.

Revelation 7:16, 17

And I heard a voice from heaven saying unto me, Write, Blessed are the dead which die in the Lord from henceforth: Yea, saith the Spirit, that they may rest from their labours; and their works do follow them.

Revelation 14:13

And he carried me away in the spirit to a great and high mountain, and shewed me that great city, the holy Jerusalem, descending out of heaven from God, Having the glory of God: and her light was like unto a stone most precious, even like a jasper stone, clear as crystal; And had a wall great and high, and had twelve gates, and at the gates twelve angels, and names written thereon, which are the names of the twelve tribes of the children of Israel. . . . And I saw no temple therein: for the Lord God Almighty and the Lamb are the temple of it. And the city had no need of the sun, neither of the moon, to shine in it: for the glory of God did lighten it, and the Lamb is the light thereof. And the nations of them which are saved shall walk in the light of it: and the kings of the earth do bring their glory and honour into it. And the gates of it shall not be shut at all by day: for there shall be no night there. And they shall bring the glory and honour of the nations into it. And there shall in no wise enter into it any thing that defileth, neither whatsoever worketh abomination, or maketh a lie: but they which are written in the Lamb's book of life.

Revelation 21:10–12, 22–27

And he shewed me a pure river of water of life, clear as crystal, proceeding out of the throne of God and of the Lamb. In the midst of the street of it, and on either side of the river, was there the tree of life, which bare twelve manner of fruits, and yielded her fruit every month: and the leaves of the tree were for the healing of the nations. And there shall be no more curse: but the throne of God and of the Lamb shall be in it; and his servants shall serve him: And they shall see his face; and his name shall be in their foreheads. And there shall be no night there; and they need no candle, neither light of the sun; for the Lord God giveth them light: and they shall reign for ever and ever.

Revelation 22:1–5

And I saw a new heaven and a new earth: for the first heaven and the first earth were passed away; and there was no more sea. And I John saw the holy city, new Jerusalem, coming down from God out of heaven, prepared as a bride adorned for her husband. And I heard a great voice out of heaven saying, Behold, the tabernacle of God is with men, and he will dwell with them, and they shall be his people, and

God himself shall be with them, and be their God. And God shall wipe away all tears from their eyes; and there shall be no more death, neither sorrow, nor crying, neither shall there be any more pain: for the former things are passed away. And he that sat upon the throne said, Behold, I make all things new. And he said unto me, Write: for these words are true and faithful. And he said unto me, It is done. I am Alpha and Omega, the beginning and the end. I will give unto him that is athirst of the fountain of the water of life freely. He that overcometh shall inherit all things; and I will be his God, and he shall be my son.

Revelation 21:1–7

Finally, brethren, whatsoever things are true, whatsoever things are honest, whatsoever things are just, whatsoever things are pure, whatsoever things are lovely, whatsoever things are of good report; if there be any virtue, and if there be any praise, think on these things. Those things which ye have both learned, and received, and heard, and seen in me, do: and the God of peace shall be with you.

Philippians 4:8, 9

For God so loved the world, that he gave his only begotten Son, that whosoever believeth in him should not perish, but have everlasting life. For God sent not his Son into the world to condemn the world; but that the world through him might be saved.

John 3:16, 17

Finally, my brethren, be strong in the Lord, and in the power of his might. Put on the whole armour of God, that ye may be able to stand against the wiles of the devil. For we wrestle not against flesh and blood, but against principalities, against powers, against the rulers of the darkness of this world, against spiritual wickedness in high places. Wherefore take unto you the whole armour of God, that ye may be able to withstand in the evil day, and having done all, to stand. Stand therefore, having your loins girt about with truth, and having on the breastplate of righteousness; And your feet shod with the preparation of the gospel of peace; Above all, taking the shield of faith, wherewith ye shall be able to quench all the fiery darts of the wicked. And take the helmet of salvation, and the sword of the Spirit, which is the word of God: Praying always with all prayer and supplication in the Spirit, and watching thereunto with all perseverance and supplication for all saints.

Ephesians 6:10–18

Now faith is the substance of things hoped for, the evidence of things not seen. For by it the elders obtained a good report. Through faith we understand that the worlds were framed by the word of God, so that things which are seen were not made of things which do appear. By faith Abel offered unto God a more excellent sacrifice than Cain, by which he obtained witness that he was righteous, God testifying of his gifts: and by it he being dead yet speaketh. By faith Enoch was translated that he should not see death; and was not found, because God had translated him: for before his translation he had this testimony, that he pleased God. But without faith it is impossible to please him: for he that cometh to God must believe that he is, and that he is a rewarder of them that diligently seek him. By faith Noah, being warned of God of things not seen as yet, moved with fear, prepared an ark to the saving of his house; by the which he condemned the world, and became heir of the righteousness which is by faith.

Hebrews 11:1–7

SOURCE NOTES

Chapter 1

1. Ken Walsh, *Sometimes I Weep* (London: SCM Press, 1973), p. 94.

Chapter 2

1. Author unknown.
2. Ken Walsh, *Sometimes I Weep* (London: SCM Press, 1973), p. 113.
3. Ibid., p. 118.

Chapter 3

1. James L. Christensen, *Contemporary Worship Services* (Old Tappan, N. J.: Fleming H. Revell, 1971), p. 90.
2. Ken Walsh, *Sometimes I Weep* (London: SCM Press, 1973), p. 97.

Chapter 4

1. Stuart Hamblen, "It's No Secret," *Reader's Digest Family Songbook of Faith and Joy* (Pleasantville, N. Y.: Reader's Digest, 1975), p. 88.

Chapter 5

1. Ken Walsh, *Sometimes I Weep* (London: SCM Press, 1973), p. 34.

Chapter 7

1. James Montgomery, "Well Done," *The Funeral Encyclopedia,* ed. Charles L. Wallis (New York: Harper & Row, 1953), p. 168.
2. Floyd Faust, *Life, Death, Life* (Nashville, Tenn.: Upper Room, 1977), p. 7.

Chapter 10

1. Harold S. Kushner, *When Bad Things Happen to Good People* (New York: Schocken Books, 1981), p. 27.

Chapter 11

1. Barry Bailey, sermon on the creation by God, First Methodist Church, June 19, 1983.

Chapter 14

1. Linda Lancaster, "Dear Abby," *Odessa American,* April 17, 1983.

Chapter 15

1. Ken Walsh, *Sometimes I Weep* (London: SCM Press, 1973), p. 115.
2. Ralph E. Hudson, "I'll Live for Him," *Hymns for the Family of God* (Nashville, Tenn.: Paragon Assoc., 1976), p. 453.

Chapter 16

1. James L. Christensen, *Contemporary Worship Services* (Old Tappan, N. J.: Fleming H. Revell, 1971), p. 89.
2. Raymond Gaylord, *Remember Me* (Grand Rapids, Mich.: Cascade Christian Church, 1978), p. 9
3. Mother Teresa, spoken when receiving Nobel Peace Prize.

Chapter 18

1. Norman Vincent Peale, *Positive Imaging* (Pawling, N. Y.: Foundation for Christian Living, 1982), p. 35.
2. Raymond Gaylord, *Dear Jonathan* (Grand Rapids, Mich.: Cascade Christian Church, 1971), p. 16.
3. "Because He Lives," Bill and Gloria Gaither (Nashville: New Benson Co).

Chapter 20

1. J. Wallace Hamilton.
2. Samuel Hinds, *The Handbook of Verse.*

Chapter 21

1. Harold Kushner, "Renewal," *Ladies Home Journal* (May, 1983), p. 48.

Chapter 22

1. E. L. Ashford, "My Task."

Chapter 23

1. John McCrae, "In Flanders Fields," *Masterpieces of Religious Verse,* ed. James Dalton Morrison (New York: Harper & Bros., 1948), p. 539.

Chapter 25

1. Martin Luther King, Jr., as quoted in *Martin Luther King, Jr.: A Documentary,* ed. Flip Schulke (New York: W. W. Norton, 1976), p. 206.

Chapter 26

1. Norman Vincent Peale, *Positive Imaging* (Pawling, N. Y.: Foundation for Christian Living, 1982), p. 35.

2. Author unknown, *Sunset . . . Sunrise,* Judy Norris, ed. (Cincinnati: Standard Pub., 1974), p. 62.
3. Alice Freeman Palmer, "The Butterfly," *A Marriage Cycle* (Boston: Houghton Mifflin, 1915).

Chapter 27

1. Raymond Gaylord, *Dear Jonathan* (Grand Rapids, Mich.: Cascade Christian Church, 1978), p. 34.

Chapter 30

1. Robert Schuller, *Move Ahead With Possibility Thinking* (Old Tappan, N. J.: Fleming H. Revell, 1967), p. 172.
2. Melvin Smith, "Tribute to Fay Smith," *Christian Caller,* January 17, 1980.

Chapter 31

1. Fred Craddock, *Sermons Preached at the Altar,* vol. 1, tape 3 (Tucker, Geo.: JBC Cassette Ser., 1983).
2. Nancy Wood, *Many Winters* (New York: Doubleday, 1974), p. 68.

Chapter 33

1. James L. Christensen, *Contemporary Worship Services* (Old Tappan, N. J.: Fleming H. Revell, 1971), p. 90.
2. Robert Schuller, *Move Ahead With Possibility Thinking* (Old Tappan, N. J.: Fleming H. Revell, 1967), p. 203.
3. Ken Walsh, *Sometimes I Weep* (London: SCM Press, 1973), p. 23.

Chapter 34

1. Nancy Wood, *Many Winters* (New York: Doubleday, 1974), p. 31.

Chapter 35

1. Norman Vincent Peale, *Norman Vincent Peale's Treasury of Courage and Confidence* (New York: Doubleday, 1970), p. 293.

Chapter 36

1. Evelyn Healey, "Journey's End," *Sunset . . . Sunrise,* Judy Norris, ed. (Cincinnati: Standard Pub., 1974), p. 7.
2. Victor Hugo, ibid., p. 1.
3. Frank E. Graeff, ibid., p. 13.
4. Alfred Tennyson, "In Memoriam," *Masterpieces of Religious Verse,* ed. James Dalton Morrison (New York: Harper & Bros., 1948), p. 372.
5. Author unknown.
6. James L. Christensen, *Creative Ways to Worship* (Old Tappan, N. J.: Fleming H. Revell, 1974), p. 223.
7. Chauncey R. Piety.
8. Christensen, *Creative Ways,* p. 224.
9. Robert Schuller, benediction used to conclude *Hour of Power* service.
10. John Henry Newman.
11. G. Edwin Osborn, *Christian Worship: A Service Book* (Saint Louis: Christian Board of Pub., 1953), p. 121.
12. Robert Schuller, *Move Ahead With Possibility Thinking* (Old Tappan, N. J.: Fleming H. Revell, 1967), p. 172.